Chapter One

On the Edge

February 2020

I WAS stood on a small grass verge with tears running down my face. My hands were gripping the railings in front of me so tightly that my knuckles had turned white, the scars from more fights than I could remember just about visible in the fading light.

'Go on then, fucking do it you coward.'

I was speaking out loud but nobody was there to hear me.

The wind was blowing hard in my face, making my eyes water, and my arms were shaking violently. I knew I must be cold, but inside I felt nothing.

Out in front of me the winter sun was starting to drop below what looked almost like the ocean's end on the horizon. The coast path stretched out in either direction but not a soul was in sight; just me and a sheer drop into what looked like an angry sea below.

I imagined my body floating, feeling peaceful for a while. Knowing what was coming but not being afraid.

Pain was ok. I had lived with pain all my life. Besides, it would be quick. Just a moment in time and then it would be done.

Vicki and the kids were back at the hotel waiting for me. I looked at my phone and there were seven missed calls and a load of messages. Every text sounded more worried than the last.

'Johnny are u ok?'

'Can you call me please?'

'Johnny this is not ok'

'The kids are worried now John, where are you?'

'Johnny answer your phone!!!!'

'I'm sat here crying John, please'

Over the last couple of days I'd been feeling more and more paranoid. We had come away to Norfolk with a load of Vicki's family, to a resort on the seafront called Potters, just down the coast from Great Yarmouth.

The kids were 15 and 12 at the time, and both had been really excited about the idea of a change of scene. East London was our home but it always seemed to be so grey and miserable. You couldn't breathe in amongst the shitty housing estates and high-rises. Everyone needed a break and here there was fresh air, the sea, a bit of open space as well as swimming pools, entertainment, and live music every night. Not that any of those things appealed to me.

I remember I had felt nervous before we set off. I just didn't feel myself. There was a tightness in my chest and a sense of anxiety in my stomach but at the same time I felt flat. Numb.

BRIGHT LIGHTS AND DARK CORNERS

THE JOHNNY GREAVES STORY

BRIGHT LIGHTS
AND DARK CORNERS

THE JOHNNY GREAVES
STORY

with **Adam Darke**

First published by Pitch Publishing, 2025

1

Pitch Publishing
9 Donnington Park,
85 Birdham Road,
Chichester, West Sussex,
PO20 7AJ

www.pitchpublishing.co.uk
info@pitchpublishing.co.uk

ISBN 978 1 83680 118 4

Typesetting and origination by Pitch Publishing

Printed and bound on FSC® certified paper in line with
our continuing commitment to ethical business practices,
sustainability and the environment.

Printed and bound in India by Thomson Press

Contents

Vicki kept asking what was wrong and I'd tell her I was knackered from work. I was doing long hours painting and decorating around London so that seemed a valid excuse. Once we had arrived, I did my usual trick of drinking until I couldn't think or feel anymore.

After a couple of days, the booze wasn't having its usual impact. I was waking up feeling tired and hungover, which then led to even more anxiety and paranoia. I couldn't cope with the people around me or the thoughts inside my own head.

I was getting more and more agitated as the days passed. I'd never thought Vicki's family liked me very much but now I was becoming really insecure. Every little comment, every look I felt they were giving me, made me feel more and more uncomfortable. Vicki and me had been together for nearly 25 years and I knew them as well as my own family, but suddenly it all felt unsteady and I wasn't sure who to trust.

We had spoken about my worries and she kept reassuring me that her family liked me, but it wasn't making any difference. In my mind, I was the outsider, the bad egg, the bloke who wasn't good enough for their daughter. Repetitive thoughts kept playing on a loop, like a scratched record:

'They think you're fucking scum.'

'They think you aren't good enough for their daughter.'

'They think you're a shit dad.'

I wanted the voices to stop but they kept on and on, over and over in my mind. Then it would escalate and I'd feel like my whole life was a failure. The idea that nobody liked me. That everyone was better off without me.

I'd made my excuses that afternoon and said I needed a walk to clear my head before dinner. That wasn't unusual for me, so Vicki had just shrugged and told me not to be too long. I wandered for maybe 20 minutes until there was nobody around and it was quiet. Maybe a bit of time away from people would help.

But the voices in my head didn't stop. They never stopped.

So I kept walking, without any idea what I was searching for. Usually it was booze or drugs but now even they didn't work. I headed along the beach and then followed the coastal path to the top of a hill that overlooked the North Sea. It was wet and muddy from the winter rain and I fell a couple of times, swearing and scrambling back to my feet, pulling myself up using the branches around me, determined to reach the summit.

As I got to the cliff edge, breathing heavily from the climb and soaked through, I noticed how cold and dark the sea looked, the last of the afternoon sun disappearing quickly. Nobody would notice if I slipped away now, would they? Maybe they wouldn't even find my body.

I wasn't scared of dying. I was more scared of living, of letting everyone down. I'd always let people down.

I looked at the phone again. Another missed call from Vicki. I put it in my pocket and stepped a little nearer the edge; the wind pushing me back as if it was trying to convince me to reconsider. I could hear my teeth chattering, through cold or adrenaline I wasn't sure.

I closed my eyes for a moment and thought about Ted and Ruby. Fuck. I collapsed to my knees, sobbing now. I just didn't want to go on. I wanted to end this here, for them. They didn't need a fuck-up of a father in their lives. Vicki could find a better man who could look after her financially. She would meet a bloke with a proper job and a few quid. My parents would be relieved too. They wouldn't have to worry about me all the time. I was a constant burden to everyone. I was pathetic. Just a pathetic excuse for a human.

I went to climb over the railings and something stopped me. I heard the sound of music from across the water and saw the disco lights from the resort. I pictured Ted and Ruby dancing and smiling, having a good time. Then I imagined someone telling them Daddy had gone. I imagined them finding my bloated, bloodied body, washed up on the beach. In my mind I pictured them screaming and falling on the sand … and a switch suddenly went in my head.

The last bit of sun had fallen below the level of the ocean and I stood and listened for the sound of their voices. For a second I thought I could hear their laughter, or maybe Vicki calling my name. I sat down on a bench and got out my phone. Another three missed calls from Vicki. I messaged her:

'Heading back now, sorry.'

Chapter Two

Born to Fight

26 years earlier – November 1984

I GREW up in a tough part of East London near Upton Park, on a little terraced street called William Worley Close. It was part of a pretty run-down estate just a stone's throw from Green Street, a busy old parade of shops and markets which ran like a boundary line between East and West Ham. At the end of Green Street, and visible from my bedroom window, towering over the rooftops, was the Boleyn Ground. This was the famous stadium that was home to West Ham United back in the day.

It was an imposing building, all orange brick, corrugated iron and barbed wire fencing. I'll always remember the noise from that place when there was a match on a Saturday afternoon or maybe Tuesday night. You could hear the crowd from our house. The chants of 'oh East Lon-don is won-der-ful', to the tune of 'When the Saints Go Marching In'. It was an ironic song the home fans would sing. Nothing was very wonderful around here.

Me and my two older brothers used to climb the fences to watch matches without paying. West Ham had been promoted back to the old First Division a few years earlier so there was a good feeling around the place and the ground would be packed with 20-odd thousand people for home games. The whole area would come to life.

West Ham was a club with a confusing identity because on the pitch they liked to play football in an elegant style. The fans almost demanded it. 'The West Ham way', they called it. But off the pitch things were completely different. The Inner City Firm or ICF were notorious and one of the most feared football hooligan groups in the country. They would meet up with rival fans and have organised fights in parks and pubs around the ground. Those fights would regularly spill on to the estate where we lived. We would stand and watch, cheering on the ICF, as punches were thrown and huge battles would take place. Afterwards, in amongst the blood and broken bottles, you would find these cards lying around on the floor that they had passed to their rivals after a good beating had been dished out.

'You have just met the ICF'.

That was football in the early 80s for you, but West Ham were definitely one of the worst offenders.

Violence was just a part of our everyday life, whether it was football fans or your next-door neighbours. If you walked up the road looking for a fight, it wouldn't take you two minutes to find one. There would always be someone there to put you in your place. This was before knife crime so people knew how to have a proper punch-up. There was almost a nobility to it. Have a fight, settle the score, move on.

Despite being a dangerous place to live in lots of ways, it could also feel like a safe haven where people stuck together. You could play football outside until late at night and leave your front door open. There was a community spirit despite the violence. People protected their own, to a point. They were usually best of friends and worst of enemies.

East London had always been an area that struggled with poverty and crime, stretching back to the rule of the Krays decades earlier, but the closure of the royal docks in the early 80s had caused a massive loss of jobs and people were on their knees. The crime rate was through the roof and people didn't seem happy. Why would they be? If you lived around here you didn't have much to smile about.

This particular Sunday afternoon, the estate was still, there was no football on and it was eerily quiet. The rooftops were covered in a blanket of mist which made it seem even more threatening than usual. Christmas wasn't far away but it wasn't feeling very festive.

Bilco, our white English bull terrier, was standing like a sentry guard by the front door. He was a big, stocky bastard with a black eye and was a legend on the estate. Mean-looking thing, but wouldn't hurt a fly. No, he wasn't what I was afraid of.

We were all sat around watching TV – I was lying on the sofa next to Mum, and my big sister Sarah and oldest brother Sam were sat opposite with Frank, who was the closest to me in age. Dad was out working as a cabbie, something he did most days when he wasn't drinking. He was a hard worker, was Dad. A breadwinner, trawling the streets of London for customers. I couldn't fault him on that front. And he could be the best dad on the planet, he really could. Sometimes he would bowl in with a bottle of ice-cream soda and a pack of sweets for us and we'd sit around the TV and listen to his stories, Dad holding court, making us laugh. But not this afternoon. This was different.

I was curled up next to Mum when the door slammed shut and you just knew straight away that something was wrong. You could feel the energy around Dad before he even appeared. It was the sound of the taxi. The way he revved the engine in the drive, the door slamming hard, his feet thudding against the driveway. He was in one of those moods.

The first thing that went through my head was whether I'd left my shoes out. Was the living room a mess? Had one of us forgotten to flush the toilet? My mind was working double quick, my heartbeat quickening. I knew Mum felt that too. I remember how her body language would shift. How her back would straighten up, her arms stiffen, that look in her eye.

'You lot, keep quiet,' she told Sarah, Sam and Frank. 'It's gonna be ok Johnny, just stay close to me.' But everything about her told me things weren't going to be ok.

Being the youngest of the four kids I was Mum's little baby boy and I idolised her. She always took real pride in her appearance did Mum. She was very slight in build, pretty with neat blonde hair. I always thought she was quite glamorous but despite that and her size, she wasn't the kind of woman to suffer any bollocks. Many a time I remember her throwing someone out of the house or standing up to a neighbour who wanted to have an argument. For a little woman, she wouldn't take any shit. One time a neighbour knocked on the door, probably with a complaint about one of us kids doing something. In fact, I dare say it was me. She was a fair bit bigger, this woman, but Mum gave her a right old slap.

At times she gave the impression of being softer and more vulnerable, but even arguing with Dad she would hold her ground and not many people did that. She was nobody's fool and had been an East End barmaid for years, so had just about seen all there was to see. She knew how to handle herself and wasn't intimidated, even by some of the notorious gangster types when she was pulling pints behind the bar. But Dad in this kind of mood was not a man to cross. You kept your head down. You stayed quiet. You did what he told you.

Bilco had given us a warning that Dad was on his way and I remember the door swinging open and seeing the look in his eye. He scanned the room and looked down at a pack of nuts that was on the coffee table.

'Who the fuck ate them?' he shouted.

Dad was a big man. Dark-haired with stubble and the best part of 18 stone.

Brazil nuts were my favourite and I had scoffed down most of them without thinking.

'That was me John, I ate the Brazils,' Mum said, lying to try to protect me.

He looked her up and down, disgusted by what had come out of her mouth. She told me to go upstairs and ushered me in that direction but I instinctively ran across the room and jumped on the sofa next to Frank. Before I had even turned around I could hear the blows landing, Mum screaming.

The four of us kids sat huddled together. Either Sam or Sarah was covering my eyes, but I had seen this many times before. I knew only too well what was about to happen.

The sounds are what stay with me the most. The noise when his fists landed on her body. The cries of pain. The thump of my own heartbeat in my chest.

I desperately wanted it to stop. I wanted to do something but I was powerless. Helpless. I wanted to cry but instead felt this huge anger welling up inside me. I could never let this happen again.

I looked at Dad as he walked away, tears of guilt running down his face, and thought to myself that one day I would get him back. I would be able to stand up to him and protect Mum.

I became a different person that day. I knew I never wanted to be in that position again. I never wanted to feel so small and weak. From that moment on I decided I would fight anyone who made me feel that way. People might hurt me but I would never let them win. If they wanted to give me another beating, I would stand there and take it. I would be a fighter and nothing and nobody would ever keep me down.

I was four years old.

Chapter Three

Learning to Lose

March 1987

I WAS eight years old when I got home from school and everything had changed. Mum was there, cleaning and keeping herself busy, but her energy was completely different. Dad was acting as though nothing had happened but his body language made it clear that the subject was not up for discussion.

We worked out over the next few days that Mum and Dad were no longer a couple. She would be there when we got home from school but as soon as we were asleep, she would leave. We started to get used to the routine – her kissing us goodnight and then within minutes the front door slamming shut and the sound of her footsteps on the pavement as she walked up the road. We later found out she was living in a small flat or hostel nearby. She had made the decision to leave her kids and this was all we got now. Our mum was gone.

We had no choice but to get on with it but inside I was absolutely broken. I didn't understand what had happened, why she had left or if there was something I had done. I was totally lost and alone. I tried to make sense of it in my head and, although I knew those fights with Dad must have been awful for her, I still couldn't work out why she would go. If I'd been better and protected her, she would have stayed. I'd let her down.

Dad was out in the cab from three in the afternoon until one in the morning, and would lie in every day rather than waking up and helping us get ready for school. Frank and me would make ourselves breakfast, find some clean uniform if there was any, pick up the dinner money Dad had left for us, and make our way to school on our own. There was nobody to take care of us. Just an eight- and nine-year-old fending for themselves. We weren't getting any proper nutrition and would spend our dinner money on sweets and chocolate. We were just living feral and staying out until all hours on the estate.

For the first couple of years, Mum would be there doing a bit of housework when we got home but it felt strange. This wasn't her house anymore. I still loved her and wanted her close, but things were different now. She seemed different too, not quite as warm. It felt as though she had moved on with her life and we weren't a big part of that. Even when she was there she wouldn't cook us a meal. Instead, she would give us some money and send us to the chip shop for dinner. We were on first-name terms with the guys in the shop because we were there almost every night.

Mum was living in a small place in West Ham Park, a mile or so away. After a while, we started to go round there once a week but it didn't last long. We would meet at the dry cleaners where she worked on Green Street after her shift and go back to her house for a meal. Then she would drop us home at 9pm and we would put ourselves to bed whenever we felt like it. Because Dad was never around, that was the only adult supervision we had during the week.

Soon after that, she started seeing some bloke called Mark. We didn't know if this was a new thing or whether it had been going on for a while. Maybe he was the reason she moved out in the first place. We didn't really care, to be honest. We had a dad and, while he wasn't perfect, we definitely didn't want another one. Mum and Mark moved to a place in Barking, which was a cab ride away, so we saw her even less after that. It was just us kids on our own, Monday to Friday, or with Dad at the weekends when he was in the mood.

He saw life in very simple terms, did Dad – spend the week grafting to support his four children and the weekend on the piss as a reward for his hard work. He did like his sport as well, to be fair, and he let us tag along if he was playing tennis or golf, but there was always drink involved. Dad did things his way and we had to fit in to that. You didn't question it. Dad wasn't a man to question.

Frank became the closest thing I had to a parent. He was only 18 months older than me and I often wondered what effect that had on him, because he was just a small kid himself, but he seemed to instinctively know how to look after me. He was my surrogate dad I suppose, because the old man just didn't have that emotional side to him. Frank was different. He could see my vulnerability, Frank. Always could.

In time, I wouldn't need much protecting from the outside world, but at eight years old I was a soft little lad who missed his mum. Frank was only nine himself but would put an arm around me and tell me everything was going to be ok. I don't know what I would have done without him, to be honest. I don't think I'd be standing here today.

My eldest brother Sam and my sister Sarah were enjoying the freedom that came with having no parents around. They didn't think about me and Frank and what we needed. They had their own issues, I'm sure. Growing up in our household, where violence was an almost daily occurrence, it was impossible to survive unscathed. But they operated in a different world, Sarah and Sam, so Frank and I did our own thing. We walked to school, had fights, wrestled, watched TV and knocked about with our mates on the estate. There was nobody to tell us to come in and get ready for bed. We never did homework because nobody made us. As long as we were asleep, or at least pretending to be, when Dad got back from work in the early hours, then there was no problem. We would do the same thing every day, on repeat.

I had been so sad when Mum had first left but, as time went on, I realised that nobody apart from Frank was going to show me any sympathy. I had to become harder, more resilient. Me and Frank started to fight a lot more. It was mostly light-hearted, pushing the sofas back and putting on boxing gloves to have a scrap. Frank would be commentating and toying with me as I was so much smaller than him but, even then, I had a lot of fight in me and never stayed down for long. I'd clench my teeth and keep throwing punches, Frank laughing and fighting back even harder until we were both exhausted and either ended up in a heap laughing or one of us, usually me, ran off in a mood.

The sensitive little boy was still alive inside me, but on the outside I became a mouthy little shit and Frank would have to be a lot tougher. He would try to act like the big brother who knew better, always needing to win the argument or have the final word. But now I was starting to hold my own.

I remember walking to primary school one day and he was getting on my nerves, telling me what I could and couldn't do. Frank was a bit taller and thicker-set than me but I just exploded with rage. I turned quickly and threw a swinging left hand which landed right on the bridge of his nose. I knew it had connected well because within a split second the blood was streaming down his face. He was crying and holding his nose, shouting at me that I was a little bastard and asking me why the fuck I had done that. He turned and headed back home to get changed, his white shirt turning redder by the second. I should have felt bad but I didn't. I just remember thinking he deserved it. I wasn't little John-boy anymore. People weren't going to walk all over me.

These moments of rage became more regular. It would always start innocently and then switch in a heartbeat. When I was made to feel small or someone took the piss, then I would get this heat building in my stomach and chest, suddenly erupting like a volcano.

The next time it happened was in the house. Frank was laughing at me and making me feel small, so I picked up this three-foot-long toy snake that I had. It was rubber on the outside with a coiled spring running through the middle, but part of it had been exposed through wear and tear. I pulled my arm back and smashed it into his body. He had no top on as we had been wrestling and the spring wrapped itself around his body and almost cut him in half. He collapsed on the floor and lay there screaming, this huge red welt appearing over his torso. He was my brother, the person who protected me and looked after me, but I felt nothing watching him in agony. That was what happened if you crossed me. I was a different person now.

Those fights with Frank were the start of something for me – an inability to control my emotions and reactions. I couldn't regulate myself or sit with the rage that built up inside of me in these moments. If I was disrespected then I hit first and asked questions later. Frank was bigger and stronger and knew he could hurt me but he never beat me. Nobody beat me because I would never give up. I'd just keep getting up and coming back for more – a bit like that robot in *The*

Terminator, whatever you do to him he just keeps reinventing himself and coming at you. I didn't know when to stop.

I never really got over Mum leaving but nothing was going to bring her back so I'd go out and get in trouble. What did it matter now? I'd fight with kids on the estate because I could. I'd even get in trouble with the police but I didn't care. Nothing mattered to me anymore, certainly not my own safety. Nobody gave a fuck about me so I didn't give a fuck about myself either, or anyone else.

Dad was blissfully unaware of this change in me because he either never saw me, or I was too scared of him to allow myself to get caught. The only time we were really together was on Sundays when he would always go down to the East Ham Working Men's Club on the edge of the estate and spend all day drinking. The working men's club was a real old-school place with wooden walls and thick carpets. Dad would be there from opening at midday until it closed late at night, sat around holding court with all his cronies and sinking 15 or 20 pints, while we all played around and hoovered up crisps and Coke.

He was a good drunk most of the time, very charismatic and charming in his own way. He would have a laugh and a joke but he could turn in an instant and become angry and violent. That's when we would be in the firing line. You couldn't moan or sulk around him. There was a code of conduct and you knew where you stood. If you crossed that line when he was drinking, then you were in for a severe beating. I'm not talking a slap either, he would really go to town on you. I'd try to run up the stairs to get away but he would always catch me. I'd curl up into a ball to protect myself and the blows would rain down.

I remember being very young when it first started. Mum wasn't there to protect me anymore and I didn't stand a chance against Dad's size and strength. I wouldn't have dared to try to stand up to him.

We had an old electric fan heater that was on the blink and he caught me putting a butter knife inside it to try to get it working. It could have been disastrous and maybe what Dad really felt was fear and a sense of protection, but he came flying down the stairs and gave me a fucking good belting. I was truly afraid for the first time in my life. Once his face went red and those big teeth came out, it frightened the life out of me. He was muscular with big strong shoulders and knew how to use his power, even on a child.

As I got older I would wear those bruises like a badge of honour. If I could take a beating from Dad and still survive, then I wasn't going to be scared of some kid at school who wanted to take me on.

Dad was never a boxer but he would go down to the Peacock Gym in Canning Town from time to time and take us with him. He liked being around fighters and talking to them, as well as watching the big fights on TV. There was an amateur club at the Peacock and I started hitting the bags and getting a bit of coaching from the guys there. I was about 11 or 12 at the time.

I quite enjoyed the training and sparring against other kids. I liked a fight anyway and when you're a kid in the amateurs you wear these big head-guards to protect you and the gloves are packed with more foam so the punches don't do as much damage.

I started to train at the East Ham and Boleyn Amateur Boxing Club on Tuesday and Thursday nights and by now I was picking up a bit of technique, learning to avoid punches as well as how to throw them. I mostly wanted to have a tear-up but I started to understand that there needed to be a method. Even then I was game and brave and didn't care about my own safety, which is not a good thing in boxing, but I wasn't scared of getting hurt. I liked pain. Pain made me feel alive. What scared me was getting knocked out or stopped in front of people. That feeling of being humiliated. I couldn't live with that.

The amateur shows would often be quite big events, usually held in working men's clubs around East London. You'd have quite a few young lads from different amateur clubs fighting each other and they would all bring friends and family, plus you'd have the regulars who attended those places every night.

There would often be a couple of hundred blokes watching, sat in chairs that had been lined up around the ring. That was before the smoking ban so everyone was lighting up. You could barely see from one corner of the ring to the other and, after the fight, you would feel like you'd smoked about 20 Silk Cut.

I had 15 or 20 of these bouts and enjoyed it, especially getting my hand raised in victory at the end, which I did a few times. I had some talent and the coaches wanted me to train more but I couldn't be arsed. I wasn't fit enough as it was and all my mates were out smoking weed and drinking on the estate. Being part of that crowd meant more to me than winning a few amateur boxing fights so I didn't commit properly and slowly started to lose interest.

I was at secondary school by this point. Langdon was a big, intimidating place with about 1,500 kids from some of the roughest areas in East London. I wasn't the type to look for trouble but I wouldn't back down if it came my way. Word had spread about me doing some amateur boxing and I would constantly have kids coming up to me and challenging me to fights.

'Think you're hard, do you mate?' they would ask.

I didn't usually have much to say in return. That was enough of a challenge for me to start throwing punches. I had a couple of fights with some lads who had a reputation as hard nuts but I more than held my own and quickly became a name. Even aged 12 and one of the youngest boys in the school, I was someone that other kids were wary of.

I never considered myself hard and I didn't want to be known as a fighter. I was only a little lad and I'm sure there were plenty of people who could have given me a good beating if they'd wanted to. I was just tough and probably a bit unhinged. I wouldn't back down from any challenge no matter who they were and I would keep coming back for more. Not because I wanted to or was trying to prove myself, but because I didn't know how to be any other way.

Frank had been my protector when we were little but now it was the other way around. He was walking home one night across the park and a group of lads approached him. Someone said something to him and was about to throw a punch when another boy jumped in.

'He's Johnny Greaves's brother. Leave him.'

The kid stepped back and Frank made it home safely. Hearing that story made me feel like I had some value. Maybe it wasn't the value I was after, which was to be liked, but that seemed to be out of reach so I had to settle for being respected and even feared. People around Upton Park knew what I was like and I suppose I started to play up to that. I couldn't seem to stop myself.

One day I had spent the afternoon with Dad and came out of the club a bit pissed. There was a shop next door and I thought I would chance my arm at buying some cigarettes. The bloke behind the counter wouldn't serve me as he knew I was underage. I regularly went in there in my uniform after school and he wasn't stupid. We ended up having a big argument, a couple of punches were thrown and next thing I knew, he chucked a mug of hot tea in my face. For a moment I stood there in disbelief, not sure what to do. Then an idea came into my head.

I sprinted round the corner to my house and picked up a baseball bat that Dad kept hidden under the stairs. I legged it back to the shop but he saw me coming and ran inside, locking the door. We stood there shouting at each other through the glass for a moment then I looked around and saw his brand new BMW sat there in the parking space outside. I'd seen him driving about in a flash motor before so I knew it was his. I lifted the bat over my head and just swung as hard as I could. Over and over again I brought the bat down with all my force, smashing the panels and the front window to pieces. He was watching from inside the shop, shouting and screaming at me to stop. I fucking beat the shit out of that car until there was almost nothing left. I remember seeing his face in the window as I walked away, looking horrified. I knew he would call the police so I left the scene sharpish and went back home, hiding the bat under my bed.

There was no way I was getting away with that and I shit myself all night, waiting for something to happen. Sure enough, later that evening the front doorbell sounded. I sat up on my bed and tried to listen to the conversation. I could hear Dad talking to them, saying it couldn't have been me as I'd been home all day with him. I felt a mixture of pride and panic. I was chuffed Dad was on my side and protecting me but at the same time I wondered what punishment he would have in store for me once that door closed. He called me downstairs and my heart sank. He stood and looked at me blankly. This wasn't angry Dad. You could always tell. He half smiled and just told me to stay away from the shop for a few weeks and keep my head down. That was Dad – you just never knew what you were going to get.

We barely saw him, never mind thought of him dating other women but one day we came out of school and he was waiting for us in his cab. That wasn't normal so straight away we were worried something was wrong and we were in trouble. He beeped the horn and gestured for us to come over. He wound the window down and in the back there was a woman in her 30s and a young boy, who was probably a couple of years younger than me. He looked shy and embarrassed. Frank and me assessed the scene for a second and then Dad piped up:

'This is Virginia and her son Martin, they are moving in,' he announced, without any emotion whatsoever.

We knew to keep quiet. Dad gave us a look as if this wasn't up for debate and we jumped in the back next to Virginia and Martin. Dad drove us home in silence, the four of us sitting awkwardly together, trying to avoid eye contact.

It had been decided that Martin would be sharing a room with us. Me and Frank would take the bunk bed and Martin would sleep on a mattress on the floor. I felt a bit sorry for the kid really but we didn't want him there. We didn't know him from Adam.

Virginia was a very slim woman and not unattractive. Apparently, she was a college lecturer and quite intelligent but it quickly became clear that she was completely incapable of anything domesticated. She couldn't cook or clean or even look after herself, never mind us or Martin. She constantly had a drink in her hand and we had heard from some guys at school that she had a bit of a reputation. There were stories of her sleeping with four or five guys at a time and now this woman and her son were living with us.

Thankfully, the relationship didn't last long. Dad and Virginia split up within a few weeks of moving in and we hoped that would be the end of it but, as they had nowhere else to live, it was decided that they would take our room and Frank and I would have to share the sofa. We couldn't wait for them to leave and thankfully that moment arrived soon enough. I got home from school one day with a mate and there she was, seemingly passed out on the sofa with an empty bottle of whisky and some perfume lying next to her along with a pack of paracetamol. She had clearly tried to take her own life and, having got through all the conventional alcohol, had moved on to the harder stuff.

We tried to move her body but she was unconscious. We had no idea what to do so called Mum and asked her to ring the police. While we waited for them to arrive, not knowing if she would live or die, we finished off the remaining cigarettes she had left. We probably should have felt a sense of panic or compassion but we were kids and didn't want her around anyway. Her wellbeing wasn't our concern.

The ambulance arrived and took her away shortly after. We got told that she had her stomach pumped and survived but what happened to her and Martin after that, I'll never know.

Home life had always been turbulent like this, and I coped with the ups and downs the only way I knew how

– fighting. Our group had become notorious among other schools and there was always a bit of needle between us. One day a few university lads from East Ham College, a big group of maybe 10 or 20 boys who thought they were smarter than us, came up to me and asked if I knew Frank Greaves. They seemed to have no idea that I was his younger brother and said they had some beef with him. Without hesitation I told them to follow me and I would find him. Instead, I led them to my gang of mates who were waiting around the corner by a block of flats. We were a good few years younger but tore into them. It was carnage and I remember the ringleader got his head kicked through a glass door. It was brutal and we never stopped to think about the consequences.

I was starting to feel like the big man around the estate but it was around this time I also became aware that something wasn't right in my head. I felt different to other kids. I knew I was angry and upset a lot of the time but I had thought that was normal. Everyone seemed that way where we lived. However, I started to notice how low I felt every day. I couldn't shift the fog unless I drank or smoked weed or got the adrenaline from a fight. Then I felt ok for a while. Or I felt something at least.

Sometimes I'd sit on my own and think about Mum and Dad. I'd get emotional, wanting Mum back and for things to be how they were but blaming myself for her leaving in the first place. The thought was always there that maybe if I had behaved or been a better person she wouldn't have gone. I had been the cause of lots of their arguments, I was sure.

She was always defending and protecting me. This was all my fault. That thought would keep coming up and then my mood would darken further until I would need to drink or smoke or fight to take away the pain.

I felt like everyone was disappointed in me. That I'd let everyone down. I would sit on my own and have a couple of spliffs to calm myself. People would ask what was the matter and I'd shrug it off. I didn't want to explain. Where I was from, if you started talking about your feelings you'd get the piss taken out of you or maybe a smack in the mouth. 'Fucking queer, sort yourself out,' they'd say. You couldn't show you were vulnerable or people would walk all over you. And I couldn't allow that. I hated myself enough as it was.

Chapter Four

Make Love and War

1996

I WAS kicked out of school at the age of 16 for a string of convictions, with fighting high on the list. I'd stolen from the school tuck shop, regularly missed lessons and was generally just a pain in the arse. I was bricking it thinking Dad would tear me apart when he found out, but he didn't seem altogether shocked and his only condition to staying in the house was that I got a full-time job.

'There's only one thing you need to know,' he said. 'Come the weekend, you owe me 20 quid.' As ever with Dad, it was delivered in a very matter-of-fact way and with the minimum of emotion. That was the deal. It was not up for negotiation.

My older brother Sam was already working in Roy's Pie and Mash shop in Queen's Market on Green Street, so he put in a word and managed to get me a job. I was hardly Gordon Ramsay but you didn't need to be, sticking a few scoops of mash on a plate and drowning it in liquor, which is a parsley sauce and East End tradition. It was a popular place though with a constant stream of people through the door, tables full of brickies and scaffolders coming in for their lunch or dinner.

The owner agreed to pay me 25 quid a week which left me with a fiver once I had paid Dad his rent. It was barely enough for a couple of beers but I didn't have any other options and I knew, for now, that I just had to suck it up and try to work out some way of earning regular money.

Life was pretty bleak from Monday to Friday, working at the shop and then sleeping at Dad's. He was always out in the cab or drinking with his mates and neither of us were very domesticated so it wasn't a particularly pleasant place to spend your time. The carpet needed a good hoover and there were empty plates and takeaway boxes strewn everywhere, not to mention the downstairs toilet that looked like something out of *The Young Ones*. So at weekends I made sure I got out of the house, usually to the pub during the day and then out clubbing in the evening. I would often have to borrow money from mates and hope someone bought me the odd drink as I was so skint.

I wasn't legally allowed to drink for another couple of years and, because of my size, I looked quite young for my age, so on nights out I would nick Frank's ID. Then I would head to the Ilford Palais, a nightclub that had a bit of a reputation for attracting a very edgy clientele. It was a big yellow-fronted building and outside there was an old fashioned sign that said 'Dancing, Dining, Entertainment'. I'm not sure about the dining but there was always plenty of entertainment. It would be full of East London faces and moody types who were all looking to mark their territory and assert some dominance. Add to that a cocktail of booze and drugs and it meant that something was always likely to kick off and I seemed to find myself in the centre of the action more often than not. I never needed a second invitation to have a fight if someone looked at me wrong or spilt my drink. I was a lot younger than most of the people there and I was never sure if I was taking on feared gang members or just Joe Bloggs from down the road, but that didn't matter to me. I would fight anyone. My safety was never a thought that entered my head.

I was skinny and slight compared to a lot of the people in those places, but I knew how to throw a punch from my battles with Frank and the amateur boxing training. I could take a shot as well. I'd had to grow up with Dad. Surrendering was never an option. My heart was never in doubt and my chin had always been pretty solid. I would regularly take on bouncers twice my size, with no real concern for the consequences.

I remember once being told to move along for no reason by some big lump outside a club. He was working the door and just wanted to throw his weight around but that was like a red rag to a bull to me. This guy was about 18 stone and 6ft-plus whereas I was 10 stone and like a midget compared to him. We had a big row and he took a step towards me. I leant back and threw a lovely long left hand that landed right on his chin. He went over like a sack of shit and everyone around just stood there, open mouthed. Then there were cheers and suddenly I was the man, people patting me on the back and offering to buy me a drink. These were the moments I craved. The feeling of being someone.

There was really nothing that scared me at that point in my life apart from my own thoughts, so I just created chaos wherever I went as a way of distracting myself. I seemed to attract trouble and would convince myself that other people were the problem, but the common denominator was me. I would find any form of conflict to stop me feeling this wave of hopelessness that threatened to wash me away.

Working in the pie and mash shop didn't do much for my self-esteem and it could be a bit embarrassing when mates who were still at school or had gone on to college popped in and saw me in my overalls and plastic cap. I had to take a fair bit of shit but in my mind it was still easier than learning algebra or trying to understand Shakespeare. In fact, it was a piece of piss and I had nobody on my back. All I had to do was heat up the frozen pie and mash, stick it in the oven and on a plate. Even a monkey could do that.

I met Vicki while working there. Her sister worked next door and I liked her the moment I laid eyes on her. She was pretty and sweet and I hadn't been around anyone like her before.

We dated for a couple of years and Vicki was still living at home at the time but, after her parents divorced, we started talking about the possibility of moving in together. I was at Dad's but he and I were starting to get on each other's tits and I needed a change. Even though I was a grown man, he still felt the need to impose himself when we were together, pushing his weight around. He had always been the alpha dog and that position wasn't up for review, despite the fact I was now 18 years old and knew how to handle myself. I would still keep my mouth shut and let him have his way but inside I could feel a growing need to assert myself and change the dynamic. I was tired of playing the little boy around him.

The moment I realised I needed to move out came one Christmas Eve. We had been down the working men's club all day, Dad, me, Vicki, Frank and his partner at the time. We'd all had a good drink up but Dad must have put away a good 13 or 14 pints and was more steaming than the rest of us put together. Frank and me were starving so made some chip butties to try to stave off the hangover for the next day, while Dad took himself off for a lie down.

We had all long since gone to bed ourselves when we heard screaming and shouting coming from downstairs. I looked at the clock and it was two in the morning. I could hear Dad banging about in the kitchen so I woke Frank and went down to see what the fuck he was playing at.

Dad was stood there in just his dressing gown and was purple with rage:

'Who the fuck left the kitchen in this state then? Hey?' He was clearly still pissed, holding himself up on the kitchen surface.

Frank was trying to be the peacemaker as ever: 'Dad, for fuck's sake calm down. We can clean up in the morning. It's Christmas, go to bed.'

'Don't you fucking tell me to go to bed, this is my fucking house,' he was shouting louder now and edging closer to Frank. I'd seen Dad in this state too many times and I wasn't going to stand here and take it.

'Fucking calm yourself down now,' I said and stepped towards him.

He looked me up and down for a second, almost confused, but sensing the challenge.

'Who the fuck are you talking to?' he stared back at me.

'You, ya cunt,' I snapped back. 'I ain't taking any more fucking shit off you.'

He was right in my face now. Nose to nose.

The girls had woken up with the noise and were stood at the top of the stairs, watching the whole thing unfold.

Dad snarled at me: 'Let's fucking go then, son.'

In a flash he whipped off his dressing gown and was stark bollock naked underneath. The girls covered their eyes in shock and me and Frank just looked at each other, more embarrassed than anything else.

But he was serious and wasn't wasting any time, stepping back and throwing a right hand that I saw coming and managed to sidestep. His balance was terrible, not helped by all the booze, and I caught him with a couple of clean shots to the head as he fell forward, then sank a punch right into his ribs. I felt the wind leave his body and he almost dropped to his knees.

Before I knew what was happening, he ran upstairs, or as fast as he could move, past the girls with his tackle flying everywhere, and reappeared with the old baseball bat that I'd used to smash up that bloke's BMW all those years earlier.

Vicki was screaming now. I was halfway up the stairs, ready to take whatever he was going to throw at me, when he lifted the bat and swung it wildly. It would have smashed my skull on impact but there wasn't enough room and the bat got caught on the wall as he tried to bring it down. It fell to the floor and we started grappling, falling down the stairs together. I was punching him in the side of the head and he was doing his best to retaliate but his reflexes were too slow.

There we were on Christmas morning, father and son going at it like teenagers in the playground. We were at the foot of the stairs now, Frank and the girls looking down from the bannister. I'd pinned him down and could feel the strength going out of him when, out of nowhere, I noticed his hand working its way inside my trouser pocket. He grabbed my bollocks and pulled as hard as he could. That was it – I let my hands go and threw a good 15 to 20 punches to every part of him I could. I was intent on causing maximum damage and he started shouting for me to stop, holding his hands up in a sign of surrender. I slowly clambered off him and collapsed on the sofa.

It was one of the most surreal moments of my life, seeing him lying there and realising what I had done. My own flesh and blood. He sloped off upstairs, cursing me as he went, and Vicki and me left as quickly as possible in a taxi. Happy Christmas, Dad.

Vicki and me spent the next day with her family and I tried my best to forget the whole thing and have a nice time but the scenes kept coming back into my mind. Was Dad ok? How badly had I hurt him? I had no idea.

I felt ashamed and embarrassed, hoping that nothing more would be said and we could just move on, but knowing that wasn't how Dad worked. We were about to settle down for Christmas lunch and my phone went. It was him. I knew he would have sobered up by then and hoped he might be full of remorse and offering an apology. He sounded serious and as though he had thought through what he was going to say:

'Son, if you think you can handle me now then we can go out in the garden and fight to the death. Come round later on and we will sort it out.'

I didn't know whether to laugh or cry. He'd had the time to consider his actions, swinging a baseball bat at the head of his own son, and this was his response. He could have the upper hand if that was what he needed. We both knew who had won and that there was a new pecking order now. I just put the phone down and decided to start looking for a new home and a new chapter in my life with Vicki.

I was still working in the pie and mash shop and barely earned enough to pay a decent rent so we ended up in a place called Manor Park, which is just off the A406 in Newham, one of the roughest boroughs in London. I was struggling for words to sum it up, so googled Manor Park and the following came up:

'Manor Park is a residential area of the London Borough of Newham in East London, England. The place abounds with shambling losers, wasters, the aged and the dumb – and broken-English-speaking refugees and dodgers of every race, colour and creed. A hovel and a ghetto at the same time. Failure hangs over the place so heavily you can taste it. Everyone else tastes it too, judging by the big gobbets of phlegm you can see gobbed out on the pavement every ten paces – the different colours inside of it are something to look at, I suppose: street art.'

To be honest, I thought that sounded pretty kind! Nobody wanted to live in Manor Park. You were only there if you had nowhere else to go. All you could hear was police sirens day and night and we lived in this filthy block of flats that you could see from all around. At least the neighbours provided some entertainment. There was a paranoid schizophrenic downstairs who would constantly shout and scream and a prostitute who would hang around at the bottom of the stairs hoping for some action.

This was not the kind of place to start a life with a new partner. It was so bad I couldn't bring myself to show Vicki the flat before we moved in. I just told her that it was good enough for now and we would make it our own in time. When she saw it herself for the first time, she nearly broke down in tears.

Our flat was on the 13th floor with a stairwell that stunk of piss and a lift that never worked. Walking the stairs every day was no bad thing though as it gave us a bit of exercise, but shortly after moving in, we found out that Vicki was pregnant. It should have been a happy time but we were both worried about the idea of bringing our new-born baby back here and carrying a pram up 13 flights of steps every day. It was going to be a disaster.

Things got even worse after Vicki's six-month scan. The doctors told us that the baby had club feet and would need multiple operations in order to live a normal life. Vicki was understandably upset and wanting reassurance but they said that until the baby was born they wouldn't know the full extent of the problem. Neither of us could imagine going back and forwards to the hospital for treatment, then having to bring the baby back to this gaff. How would we live here with a disabled child? How would we cope? I was desperate to find a way of bringing in more money to give us a better life but had zero qualifications and no training.

I'd never really thought about making money from fighting but I had started to go and train every now and then at the Peacock Gym, the place my old man had taken us to as kids. Some of the biggest names in boxing had spent time there down the years – Sir Henry Cooper, Sugar Ray Leonard, Frank Bruno, Prince Naseem Hamed, Lennox Lewis and Floyd Mayweather. It had a name and a reputation as a proper boxing gym, full of characters and tough-looking lads who clearly knew how to handle themselves. You never knew who you were going to bump into down there or whether bumping into them was a good idea. Even getting to the gym meant keeping your wits about you. Past the steel works and disused industrial wastelands, under the graffiti-covered flyover, Canary Wharf the other side of the railway tracks but seeming like a different world entirely.

The gym itself had a little cafe as you walked in and then some weights and fitness equipment with a room at the back for a boxing ring. You'd have these huge Eastern European weightlifters mixing with people off the street and then the sound of boxers hitting the pads or leather on skin when sparring was in full swing. People would be sat around wrapping their hands, skipping, looking in the mirror shadow boxing, circuit training. There was a real vibe in there and you could feel the boxing history.

A few of my mates would knock about there. A lot of London taxi drivers would use it as a base to come in and do a workout and then head off to the West End for a shift. Frank was a cabbie himself and some of our friends had gone into that line of work so I would go and see them for a cup of tea and a chat and then maybe work up a little sweat. I'd bring some trainers and a pair of shorts and hit a bag for half an hour or so, maybe ten minutes on the treadmill on special occasions. I was a million miles from the level of professional boxers or even talented amateurs who would frequent the place. You'd get some really good fighters in there, British title holders and all sorts. I was just a skinny little prick from Manor Park who thought he was tough but, in there, I kept my head down and knew my place.

I was usually knackered from work and could barely be bothered to go but home wasn't the most appealing place to be and sometimes hitting the bag relieved a bit of the tension and anger I was feeling. Life already felt like a challenge but it was going to get even harder pretty soon. The doctors still couldn't give us any guarantees about the baby and its condition, and Vicki was understandably worried and tired a lot of the time. I was numbing out my feelings with work, the odd fight in the street or in a pub, a fair bit of booze and the odd gram of cocaine when I could get my hands on it.

On this one occasion, I'd got into a fight in some pub on the Friday night. The next day, I was covered in cuts and bruises as I headed to the Peacock for a workout. An old friend of mine walked in, took one look at me and we got chatting about my fighting habit. He started telling me about the unlicensed boxing game and how I should give it a go. Apparently, you didn't have to pass any test or have any qualifications. There was nobody to tell you if you were good enough or not. This was a world for people who liked a scrap and were prepared to take on anyone for a few quid at their own risk. He told me I could earn four or five hundred pounds for a night's work. That was more than I was getting for a week of work and, if true, would give me, Vicki and the baby a chance of a life away from Manor Park. I was already sold on the idea.

If you've ever watched the likes of Anthony Joshua or Tyson Fury on a big televised boxing show, that is very much the other end of the spectrum from the unlicensed game. Professional boxing is governed quite strictly: all the fighters have to be licensed and there is a lot of emphasis on the health and safety of the boxers. Many of the shows are on television and the fighters are, on the whole, proper athletes. Unlicensed boxing, by comparison, is a bit like the Wild West. These are no professionals and you don't need a licence to box. The British Boxing Board of Control (BBBC) wouldn't give half of these people the time of day, never mind sanction them to fight on a proper show. This was underground boxing more akin to something you would see in *Fight Club*. It was a place for people who liked a punch-up and needed money. Born out of the bare-knuckle game, made famous by the likes of Lenny McLean and Roy 'Pretty Boy' Shaw, the fighters and promoters could get away with a lot more than they would in a sanctioned fight.

I got the number of a bloke called Alan Mortlock, who was a bit of a name in the unlicensed boxing scene, and we arranged to meet in a pub near the gym one night. Alan was an unusual character – stocky, muscular and with a shaved head but quite a calm, thoughtful manner that didn't really match his appearance. He had a presence about him that you knew he'd seen and done some things in his time but he told me that he was now a born-again Christian. He would pray with the fighters before they went in the ring, which seemed a bit odd. He made his living from setting up fights between blokes with no real experience who didn't train properly and were taking their lives into their hands in the name of entertainment, then he was praying for them.

As the story goes, he had previously drunk more than 100 pints of strong lager a week, and was close to going off the rails, but had then turned his life around through boxing and God. He was known as the 'pirate promoter' by the boxing authorities because he went under the radar and did things his way. They didn't approve and there had been lots of attempts to stop it from happening but people were willing to pay to see the fights, his events were often sold out, and there were enough people like me who were willing to get their face punched in for money. Mainly East End tough guys, bouncers, and unofficial debt collectors.

Alan seemed a nice enough fella and we got on quite well. He asked what I weighed and it turned out there was a space for me on a show that weekend, if I fancied it. Of course I fucking fancied it! So that was that. No contract, no medical, no fitness test, nothing. I think we even had to sign a waiver saying if anything happened in the ring then we were responsible for our own health and safety. It didn't fill me with confidence but I'd been to some unlicensed fights in the past and most of the fighters didn't look that good to me. I wasn't anything special either but had a bit of natural talent, some experience in the amateurs, and I was tough. There was no situation I hadn't been in and I had no fear. I'd faced the old man as a child, the toughest kids in the area, mobs with baseball bats and gangs with knives – this would be a walk in the park compared to that, surely?

Chapter Five

Fighting for a Future

January 2004

MY FIRST fight was at the world famous York Hall in Bethnal Green, where a lot of the big professional boxing shows took place. I'd been to a few events there with Dad and Frank growing up and it was a great venue. Quite small but really intense with everyone close to the ring and an overhanging balcony that people would lean off and scream their support during fights. At those professional boxing shows the atmosphere was always a bit moody, with loads of wannabe boxers coked off their eyeballs and usually a few crowd fights during the evening, but this was a level beyond even that.

I went down to the changing rooms and was initially hit by the smell of sweat and BO. But that was nothing compared to the air of intimidation about the place. There were a few gangsters walking about and hardened criminals. Half of this lot were probably on Interpol's most-wanted list.

These cramped little meeting rooms had been turned into changing areas and were packed with fighters having their hands wrapped, shadow boxing, getting wound up by their mates, most of whom were masquerading as trainers and coaches. I remember one bloke was warming up on the pads and had a bit of confidence about him. On his shorts it read 'The Guvnor' and I had a little smile to myself. The guy clearly ate well and didn't do much training, judging by the belly hanging over his shorts. He seemed to know everyone though and was commanding a bit of respect.

'You been doing this a while?' I asked him.

'I'm the fucking world champion mate,' he replied, looking me up and down.

Turns out it was Jason 'The Guvnor' Giver. If he was a world champion then I felt confident I'd be able to hold my own.

I got changed alone and kept myself to myself. I just wanted to get in the ring and get it over with. I was fighting a guy called Phil Lashley who I didn't know much about but I stopped him pretty easily and knew straight away that this was a level I could operate at. These lads weren't anything better than I had taken on in bars and clubs and most of them lacked the technique to really box, something I had picked up in the amateur game. Within weeks I had won seven or eight fights and was making my way up the rankings.

The extra money was a godsend and allowed me and Vicki to buy some things for the baby and do up the flat a little bit. Not that I would declare all my earnings to Vicki. I would hand over the cash to her after a fight, less some money for beer and coke. That was my secret and I felt I deserved it if I was the one putting my life on the line.

Our first child, Teddy, was born on St George's Day in 2005. He looked healthy and well in himself which was a huge relief, but his feet were pointing backwards and clearly something wasn't right. Within 12 weeks of being born, they had operated on him, cutting and stretching the tendons in his legs and then putting them both in plaster casts. It was horrible to see your own flesh and blood, so small and innocent, having to go through that. He didn't seem to be aware of what was happening but it was traumatic for Vicki, especially.

Over the next few months we were in and out of hospital so they could operate and try to correct the bone structure. I was working during the week and fighting most weekends but for Vicki he was her only focus, day and night. She was worried about whether he would be able to walk, spending her time sleeping on hospital floors or dodging the crazies back at our block of flats. I just did the best I could to support her, all the while trying to keep myself and my own issues in check. That was hard enough in itself.

We needed all the money we could get our hands on if we were going to find a way out of Manor Park, so I became a regular on the unlicensed scene, but keeping my nose clean wasn't easy. You had to play the game and understand who was paying your wages. I think it was a bit of a racket for a lot of these London faces and you did as you were told. There was one night when the promoter made it clear I wasn't there to win.

'Just lose the fight and I'll double your money,' he said, brazenly.

I had never taken a backwards step in my life and I certainly wasn't used to losing fights so I took a second to think.

'How do you work that out then?' I said, glaring at him.

'Do what you have to do, I don't care,' he replied, coldly. 'Just don't win and it's double bubble. Yes or no?'

He didn't seem like someone to fuck with and I needed the cash, so I reluctantly agreed.

My training for the fight game had largely been done on school playgrounds or outside the kebab shop in the early hours of the morning. I'd like to say that the unlicensed game knocked a few of the rough edges off but I think it added a few as well. This is where I learned to hold, grab people by the bollocks, bite, head-butt. Whatever it took to stay alive.

I was building bad habits and drugs were a part of that. Coke, mainly, although I wasn't fussy. I was around it so much that I even started selling a bit here and there. I knew a few people who liked a dabble, so there was easy money to be made. I would knock out ten 'tickets', slang for pills or coke, and that would be extra money that I didn't have to tell Vicki about. Money that would continue to feed my habit.

I got to know some of the people who dealt the stuff on a bigger scale and they let me put a few of my deals on the slate. That meant I could pay the money back when it was convenient for me. Before I knew what I was doing, the amount I owed was out of control. At one point it got as high as £4,000 and I had no way of paying it back. These guys wouldn't think twice about sticking a hole in you or worse, so when I got a call one day asking where the money was, I panicked. I didn't have £4,000. The only person I knew with that kind of dough was Dad but no way was I asking him. He'd have killed me himself.

I'd been getting some decent results in the ring, beating some reasonable fighters, and the chance came up to fight for the British title. That sounds more glamorous than it is, especially in the unlicensed game, but the money would be more than I was used to getting and came in the nick of time. I made a few calls and explained the situation to my contact in the underworld. I said I was going to be earning a decent wedge for this fight and would make sure all that cash was paid to them as soon as the bout was done. He agreed but made it clear to me that unless I kept my word, there would be consequences.

Now I just had to negotiate the fight. Winning or losing didn't matter, just get the money and get out of there.

My opponent was Matty Leonard, a London fighter who sold a load of tickets and had a good record. I'd seen him on a few bills in the past. He was a tough man and an ex-professional boxer, so he knew how to fight. I think he had been in a bit of trouble with the law so had given up the professional game and was making a few quid on the unlicensed scene, where he was a level above most fighters.

Despite my worries outside the ring, I felt a million dollars physically that night. I was confident and on my toes from the start. The run of victories had instilled some belief in me and I fancied myself for the win. This was my biggest fight so far and within 30 seconds I threw the best four-punch combination of my life. I looked up, expecting to see him flat on his back, but there he was, stood right in front of me. He looked at me and smiled.

'You punch like a fucking tart,' he said.

He was simply too strong, too tough, and too experienced for me. He would overpower me in the clinches, push me around when we got up close, and began to wear me down as the fight went on. I had never boxed more than four rounds before and this was an eight-round contest.

My training had never been the most intense so I was blowing hard, feeling weaker by the round. He was landing more and more regularly and I could feel the snap in my own shots start to fade as the fatigue set in. A couple of times I was dazed but hung on for dear life. The crowd were starting to smell blood and, the further the fight went, the more I was fading. I knew this feeling well. I could see Dad standing over me with his teeth showing, red-faced and full of rage. Me, helpless on the floor, taking punch after punch.

I had never quit then and I wasn't about to now. There was no way I was giving up. I'd take my beating if I had to. But in the last round he landed five or six clean head shots, none of which I saw coming. The rule in boxing is that you must defend yourself at all times but I didn't have the energy to even hold my hands up. The referee stepped in to save me from further punishment and, while a little part of me was relieved, I was also heartbroken. Genuinely heartbroken. I had thought I was the toughest man in Britain up until that point but here I was, being helped out of the ring, concussed and confused.

Matt had given me a real working over and I was covered in bruises, my eyes closing and looking like I'd been hit by a number five bus. I was lost in the moment, feeling a mixture of physical pain and self-loathing. But as I walked back to the dressing room, I noticed the crowd were giving me a really warm reception. People were on their feet and applauding, patting me on the back. They recognised how much of a fighter I was and, for a moment, the clouds lifted. Then I remembered the drug debt. Everything I had gone through to earn this money, every bump and bruise I would feel in the morning, was for nothing. I made the call and reluctantly handed over all the money.

Despite clearing my debts, things were still really tight at home with a new-born baby to support, as well as my drug habit on the side, and I needed all the money I could get my hands on. I would always ring Alan and see what shows he had on and whether there was a space for me. I didn't care where it was or who the opponent might be. I would fight anyone and put together another decent run of wins that took me all the way to the British title.

I was carving out a decent reputation in the unlicensed game but one bout against a guy called Roger Brotherhood became my ticket into the professional boxing arena. I put in a really good performance that night, showing skill and plenty of character, going through the full repertoire and entertaining the crowd.

One of Roger's old stablemates was a guy called Carl Greaves, who was an ex-British champion. He had been a really good fighter, had fought on some big TV shows and been in some real barnstorming fights, including a classic against Alex Arthur that people still talk about today. I didn't know it at the time but he was ringside during the fight and came up to me afterwards.

'I'm a fan of yours Johnny, really nice to meet you,' he said.

Nobody was a fan of mine so I was sceptical straight away but he seemed like a genuine bloke. He spoke in a thick Nottingham accent and still looked fit from his fighting days, wearing a sharp-looking suit and with his blonde hair slicked back.

'You looked good in there, Johnny. You can fight a little bit. Listen, I've just started managing some professional fighters and putting on shows. Have you ever thought about going pro?' he said.

I told him that I had never thought I was good enough but enjoyed the unlicensed fights and was up for anything if a pound note was involved. He said he wanted to swap numbers but I didn't believe anything would come of it.

Maybe he was pissed up and just being friendly. You got a lot of those types at boxing shows.

I thought I couldn't be a professional boxer in a million years. If he had any idea what I was really like then he would never have suggested such a thing. I was doing alright in the unlicensed game but physically and emotionally, I was a mess. There was nothing professional about me. I left that night and didn't give it any more thought.

The next day I had a phone call from a number I didn't recognise. It turned out to be Carl and he was serious about me turning professional. We talked about the possibility of fighting on the road and he had to explain what that meant.

'Look Johnny, professional boxing works two ways. You're either a ticket-seller and make money for the promoter, in which case you get to win fights. If you don't sell tickets but can look after yourself a bit, you become an opponent and fight to lose,' he explained.

I'd sold a few tickets for unlicensed fights but it was a massive pain in the arse. You were constantly calling and messaging people, trying to convince them to come and watch you. Then you'd be driving around to collect the money and they would let you down at the last minute. It was a full-time job and I already had one of those plus a missus and kid at home.

I asked what kind of money I would make for fighting on the road and he told me I could earn as much as £1,500 a time. That was significantly more than I was getting in the unlicensed game, almost three times more, and would be a game-changer for me and Vicki. I sent off all the forms and kept my fingers crossed. There is never a guarantee that the BBBC will grant you a licence, particularly when you've come from the unlicensed game, which has a bit of a stigma attached to it. They will look at your record and maybe even watch some videos as well as doing a health check. For now, it was just a pipe dream.

While I was waiting for my interview with the board, something happened that threatened to derail my hopes of turning pro. Not just that, but it would put my ability to be a partner and father in jeopardy as well.

Vicki and I had been invited to the wedding of a family friend. It was a mid-summer day and red hot outside, so I wasn't sure what to wear. Frank was going suited and booted but Vicki convinced me it was ok to wear a pair of smart shorts. I knew a lot of the people who would be going so wasn't too worried, but when we arrived it was clearly a bit more upmarket than I had imagined and the shorts didn't go down well at all.

I was already feeling paranoid about my outfit but a lad called Tim, who I knew a little bit through a connection with Dad, decided to get stuck into me. There was all kinds of banter flying around, most of it light-hearted, but he had an edge about him and wouldn't let it lie. He would walk past and make little comments or join in when I was chatting to some of the lads I knew and start taking the piss. He was really winding me up but I was doing my best to ignore it.

The booze was flowing and Vicki had gone overboard on the champagne. By the end of the night she was feeling unwell and I went outside to sit with her. I was pulling back her hair as she was sick, telling her it was going to be ok and trying to arrange a taxi home. At that point, Tim wandered past and made a comment about Vicki not being able to handle her drink. I wasn't having any more of it.

'Tim mate, shut your fucking mouth or I'll knock you out,' I spat.

He looked embarrassed in front of his mates and I thought that might be the end of it. He knew I boxed a bit and didn't seem the type to take it any further. I turned back to look after Vicki but the next thing I knew I could feel his weight on my shoulders. He had jumped on me and was clinging on, landing punches to the side of my head. People were still filing out of the venue and suddenly there was a huge commotion. Some of the lads piled in and managed to prise him off me and held us both back but I was seething and managed to get myself free. I walked straight over to him, landing a huge left hand that caught him flush in the face. His nose exploded and he was unconscious before he hit the floor, swaying and landing face first on the concrete. There were screams and gasps and time seemed to stand still for a moment.

His face looked an absolute mess and he wasn't moving. Fuck. I was panicking and people were shouting and rushing to see if he was ok. A group were gathered around him, propping up his head. There were cries from a few of the women who obviously knew him well and the rest of the people were just trying to leave as quickly as possible. I was dragged off by a couple of blokes I didn't recognise and just slumped down next to Vicki, who was sobering up fast.

Within what seemed like minutes I could hear the sound of the Old Bill arriving. I was put in handcuffs and taken off to Chelmsford Police Station. For the next 20 hours or so, I sat in the cells and cried my eyes out. I hadn't just ruined my life, I had ruined Vicki and Teddy's lives as well. I was going down for this, it was a definite bang-up job, and they would be left in that horrible flat with nobody to support or look after them. Even if I got let off with a short sentence, I would lose my job. Nobody would employ me. Any chance I had of being a professional boxer was down the shitter as well. If the board found out about this they would throw my application in the bin. It was frowned upon for any fighter to use his fists outside the ring. My life was fucked.

I was allowed out on bail the next day and a court date was set. I had six months to plan my defence, to make plans for my likely imprisonment, and there was a decision to make over my boxing application. I decided to keep quiet and blag it. Maybe there was a chance they wouldn't find out. It seemed a long shot but I had to give myself a chance of earning money if I ever got out. I might be going away for a long time.

I was given legal aid and put in touch with a lawyer called Anthony Cole. He told me the case against me was focused on two things. Firstly, the damage that had been inflicted.

It had only been a single punch but Tim's cheekbone had been shattered and needed surgery to rebuild. There was also a big slash across his face.

Secondly, the prosecution were alleging that I had stamped on his head when he was on the floor. I'd been a bit pissed at the time but I knew myself and that wasn't something I would do. So we set about finding some defence witnesses, people who would testify as to what happened. They were my only hope, along with a judge who might take pity on me, but I wasn't confident. In fact, I had already resigned myself to time inside.

For the next six months it was all I thought about. I spoke to Frank about supporting Vicki and Teddy, making sure there would be enough people around them to help financially. Frank was amazing as always, reassuring me that I would be ok, telling me that he would step up if needed.

I had heard nothing from the BBBC. Maybe they wouldn't find out until it came to trial. So I continued with the licence application process, travelling to London Bridge for my interview and meeting them in a strange little room above a pub. It felt like I was in court already, all these board members sat around this big table, grilling me about my amateur boxing career, training schedule and ambitions in the ring. It was really hard work but I did my best to answer the questions, all the while fearing that it was futile. If I got sent down I wouldn't be boxing anyone, never mind getting a licence.

I must have passed the first part of the test because I got a letter telling me they wanted to see me have a full-contact spar at the Peacock Gym. It would be against an opponent of their choosing and a couple of board members would be ringside to assess. If they were happy with what they saw, I would be getting my licence. That was the easy part for me. Fighting was the one thing I was comfortable with and, having fought guys like Lee Purdy and Tom Glover in the unlicensed game already, lads who had been talented pros, a little spar held no fears for me. I sailed through it and I think they were impressed. They told me afterwards that I would be getting my papers in the post.

'Welcome to professional boxing,' one of the guys said, and smiled.

I was momentarily happy, the adrenaline still working its way through my body. But my mind quickly returned to the court case. This was all meaningless. My boxing career was going to be finished before it even started.

The court date seemed to take an age to arrive but by the time it did I had resigned myself to at least a couple of years behind bars, maybe more. I would miss Teddy's first steps. Vicki would probably find someone else. Why would she wait? I was a criminal. A thug. Even if she waited, what prospects did I have? What could I offer her?

My lawyer wasn't particularly confident. The defence witnesses might be able to clear me of any stamping but the injuries were still awful. Our case was centred around self-defence and good character, citing my work with the amateur boxing club and some good references. That was about it. I gave Frank one last call and made sure he was ready if I got sent down. I couldn't have Vicki and Teddy coming back to the flat on their own.

I was advised to bring a toothbrush and some clothes. In my mind I was as good as down. The trial took place at Chelmsford Crown Court. It was a horrible place and had the look and feel of a prison from the outside, with this heavy red-brick exterior and blacked-out windows. I'd worn a suit and tried to make myself look presentable. Vicki and all my family were sat in the public gallery behind me, fearing the worst.

I hadn't known exactly what to expect or how long it would last but the biggest shock was when they showed the pictures of Tim after the assault. It was horrific and looked like he had been beaten up by a gang carrying bats or knives. They showed the aftermath, pictures of Tim in hospital and during his recovery. There was no way the judge would let me off after seeing that. I wouldn't have shown me any pity if I'd been in his seat either.

After both sides had pleaded their case, the moment arrived. The judge stood up to pass sentence and I just looked down, resigned to my fate. 'John Greaves, I hereby sentence you to two years' imprisonment.'

Fuck. There it was. Two years on the inside. Maybe a bit less with good behaviour but a long stretch nonetheless. I was finished. Me and Vicki were finished. My heart almost stopped beating in my chest and then the tears came.

He continued:

'.... suspended for two years.'

I looked up and then to my lawyer, who raised an eyebrow and smiled. I could hear the cries of relief from Vicki and my family in the seats behind me. I breathed out slowly, still trying to take it in. The judge was still talking but now I was only half-listening. There was a £2,000 fine and 250 hours of community service. I didn't care about that. I was free. I didn't know how but I was free. I shook my lawyer's hand and gave Vicki the biggest hug. We just stood and sobbed together as the courtroom emptied.

For the next year I spent every Sunday working at the Indian temple on Green Street, painting and doing general maintenance. That was my punishment and it was brutal, especially as most Saturday nights I was on the piss and coked off my eyeballs, but it was a lot better than being in prison. I still had my freedom. I still had Vicki and Ted.

And because the board appeared to be unaware of my case, I was still a professional boxer in waiting.

Chapter Six

Thrown to the Lions

9 June 2007

Fight 1

Rob Hunt v Johnny Greaves
Eston Sports Academy, Middlesbrough

I had 48 hours' notice. In two days' time I was to make my debut as a professional fighter and I was shitting myself. I'd got the call to fight a lad called Rob Hunt and, without knowing anything other than the weight and the fee, had agreed to fight. I'd had more tear-ups than I could remember and a load of unlicensed bouts, but I had no idea how that would compare to professional boxing and I was scared. Terrified, actually.

I was doing bits and pieces of building work at the time so hadn't been training too hard and I'd been on the piss most of that week so I wasn't on top of my game, either.

I headed to Euston on a packed tube train, leather bag over my shoulder containing everything I needed to fight – gloves, gumshield, shorts, boots and a towel, along with a sausage roll, some crisps and a couple of cans of lager for the journey. There is no private jet at this level of professional sport. No fancy coach with heated seats and widescreen TVs. No, I was on my own. Five hours sat in the economy class of some stinking train to Middlesbrough, with a load of football fans and families.

So much was running through my mind. Was I good enough? Would I be knocked out? Would I even find the place?

The journey was painful and a world away from my usual routine. I had grown up and lived in East London all my life and didn't make a habit of leaving the area. Not because I liked it or felt any kind of connection with the place. To be honest, it was a dump but it was all I had ever known and I didn't make enough money to be jet-setting off to anywhere more glamorous. So even a trip to the north-east of England felt like a bit of an adventure, although not one that I was very excited about.

Three hours into the trip and I had no idea where I was. The names of the stops weren't familiar and it was making me anxious. I wondered if I could get away with a fag in the toilet to calm the nerves.

This was going to be a decent payday and one that I badly needed, so I decided I'd have to suck it up rather than get booted off the train and be stranded in the middle of nowhere.

I just sat staring out the window and imagining what was in store for me.

We stopped at Stevenage and Darlington, and then finally arrived in Middlesbrough.

My first impression was it smelled like shit. There were these giant chimneys billowing out smoke like it was Chernobyl. I was used to working-class towns but this was another level – all greasy spoon cafes, betting shops, boarded-up houses and pubs that had clearly seen better days. It was also about minus five degrees as I walked from the station and asked a couple of people where Eston was. I could barely understand what they were saying but worked out it was a little place on the edge of the main town centre.

Eventually I found the venue – Eston Sports Academy. I wasn't expecting Wembley Stadium but this was still a bit of a comedown. It was a bloody leisure centre and when I turned up at about 1pm there were still mothers taking their kids swimming and no sign of any boxing whatsoever.

I had a quick fag outside and got chatting to some bloke who told me that later on they would turn the gymnasium into a boxing arena, with a few hundred people expected. I wandered inside and presumed someone might be waiting to greet me or even know who I was, but there was nobody around and no sign of life. I managed to find my way to a little check-in room around the back of the building that had a set of scales and a few bits of boxing apparatus lying around. The bloke looked at me blankly:

'What's your name, lad?' he asked.

'Johnny Greaves,' I replied.

'Mmmm, no, can't see you down here mate,' he said, looking confused. He was gazing down at the list of fighters in front of him.

'Who you fighting?' he asked.

'Rob Hunt,' I replied, starting to lose my patience.

'Oh right, here you are. You're in a changing room with the other away fighters. Should be on about four o'clock. See you later.'

Welcome to big-time boxing.

I thought the unlicensed game had been a bit rough and ready but this was no better. The dressing room was poxy too. There was water on the floor, one leaky shower and about seven fighters in there, all getting changed together.

The away fighters were generally a bunch of blokes who were there to lose. It's a bit like in ancient Rome when the Christians got thrown to the lions. The home fighters were the guys who had sold all the tickets and were deemed to have some talent. We were the scum who were there to make up the numbers. As far as the organisers and supporters were concerned, they were hoping we would get knocked out. Our view was a bit different – we would give our all and fight hard but we had chosen this route as an easy payday and knew our role: give some young prospect a bit of a workout, keep out of the way of any big shots, probably lose on points but take home a wedge of cash and fight again next week.

We were known as journeymen and boxing has always needed them to survive. Without us, the young prospects would have to start their careers by being thrown in with really good fighters who might know a bit too much for them. Promoters wanted to ease their young fighters into the sport, have a little move about with a journeyman, learn the game slowly. But they wouldn't want them to lose because that would look bad. They wanted their prospects to have unbeaten records because that made them appear unbeatable and therefore more marketable.

The unknown for the journeyman was always how good your opponent might be. He could be a future world champion for all you knew. Or he might be some hyped-up nightclub bouncer with a big following who was making lots of money for the promoter. Ultimately, we didn't really care as long as the money was right and frankly I would have fought Mike Tyson for a thousand quid. But there was an element of jeopardy. Were you fighting someone who couldn't punch their way out of a paper bag or the next Tyson Fury in waiting?

Thankfully, my manager Carl Greaves had made the trip to offer some moral support. I call him a manager, and to most serious boxers he is, but in my world he was a guy who took a phone call and, unless it was the Incredible Hulk wanting to fight me, said yes. Even then I'd give it a go for the right money.

I got changed into my boxing shorts and boots and Carl, who hadn't long stopped professional boxing himself and still looked as if he was fit enough for a few rounds, taped up my hands before a little warm-up on the pads. There was no space as the changing room was packed with other boxers so we had to find a corner of the piss-soaked toilet area. Carl was in a t-shirt with 'Team Greaves' on the back, a nice touch but not something that would mean anything to anyone except me and him, and was offering a few words of encouragement as I practised little combinations.

'Just have a look early on, keep on your toes and out of the way of any big shots. Take your time, don't get caught, not too much bravado. Do a job and we will get you back on the road next week,' he was saying keenly, as my punches landed on the pads he was holding.

I wasn't really listening. I had too much adrenaline running through my body and was taking it out on the pads, throwing big punches like I meant business.

It was a Sunday afternoon dinner show and I was third or fourth on the bill. A daytime dinner show meant that you had a load of local sorts on the booze all day, wanting to see someone get their head caved in. Ideally, the scrawny little gobshite from London.

I was up and down like a yoyo. One minute sat with my head between my legs contemplating what lay ahead, the next bouncing around shadow boxing, then laughing and bantering with the other fighters, pretending that I wasn't worried. A few other lads came back in bloodied and bruised. One poor bloke had been properly knocked out and was really groggy. It was a horrible place to be, like going to the gallows but not knowing if you might be spared. Eventually someone poked their head around the door.

'Johnny, you're on.'

I had a brand new pair of sequinned shiny shorts and silky jacket. I really looked the part. But I was nothing more than a journeyman – have gloves, will travel. I wasn't here to beat anybody. That wasn't going to happen. This was solely about survival and if I could make the opponent look good along the way, then even better. That would keep the promoter happy and the punters buying tickets for his next show. It's a bit of a con really but that's how small-hall boxing works. We all knew why we were there and it wasn't to win. I could have beaten half the kids I fought but, if I had, the phone would have stopped ringing and this was my way of making a few extra quid. Not a lot, mind you. By the time you'd paid your travel expenses and maybe a local face to stand in your corner and pour water down your throat between rounds, you probably walked away with five hundred quid in your pocket. Not much for getting punched in the face.

My stomach was starting to churn. I didn't care about pain, I was used to that. I just didn't want to be knocked out and humiliated. I couldn't bear the idea of travelling back home and having to tell Frank, Vicki and Mum and Dad that I'd got smashed up and stopped. I couldn't handle that.

My opponent, Rob Hunt, had fought four times and managed four wins. He had also sold all the tickets for this show. Nobody had bought a ticket to watch Johnny Greaves, clearly. Why would they?

Hunt was a big, tall lad with muscles and a six-pack. I knew this because I had been given a programme on the way in and he was the cover photo, all oiled up and looking ready for action. That was the first time I had seen my opponent. I wasn't one for research or preparation. That just made me more nervous.

Because he was the headline act, he would enter the ring last. The opponent always comes out first and then has to wait around in the ring getting cold while the fighter with all the support takes his time and the announcer whips up the crowd. It's just a part of boxing and designed to increase the tension.

My name got called out: 'From East Ham, Johnny … Greaves.' A chorus of boos followed.

I'd always been known as John but had decided to call myself Johnny and create a kind of persona. I wanted to be a bit of an entertainer in the ring. I was a miserable bastard in real life. A depressive, downbeat, mouthy little fucker. This would be a completely different me. Nobody needed to know what I was really like or the thoughts that occupied my head.

I remember the look of real hatred on people's faces as I walked into the hall. Most of them were pissed up on cheap lager and coked up to their eyeballs. The abuse was shocking, even to me, and people were acting like they wanted to come in the ring and knock me out themselves.

I knew that shit was about to get real. I was 300 miles from home with no trainer and no support. Nobody gave a fuck about me and whether I lived or died. I didn't care about that much either but the thought of being humiliated, knocked out in front of all those people: that was worse than the thought of dying. The idea of being exposed for what I was – a nobody.

Hunt got introduced and the crowd went crazy. It was dark inside the hall now apart from the lights that illuminated the ring. Rows of chairs had been lined up on each side but most people were standing ready for action or making their way back from the bar with pints in hand.

I was bobbing up and down on my toes, trying to ignore all the noise and keep my focus. I caught him walking to the ring out of the corner of my eye. He was lapping it up, saluting the crowd and getting fist bumps from people he seemed to know. I looked around and everyone was baying for blood. 'Fucking kill him Rob!' I heard someone scream.

He got into the ring and gave me a glare, punched his gloves together and put his gumshield in. He looked confident, like he was here to do a job.

I had less muscle and a smaller frame but I tried to ignore the size difference and threw a few air punches, shots I probably wouldn't be throwing in the fight. The referee pulled us together and Hunt seemed even bigger up close. Naturally taller and broader and obviously a lot fitter than me, although that wasn't saying much.

The opening bell rang and I was determined to shut the crowd up. I swaggered to the centre of the ring and started dancing around, pulling faces. That was until the first punches landed. He threw a couple of shots which didn't seem to have that much power behind them but in the professional game you wear eight-ounce gloves. They are much smaller and have less padding on them than normal gloves so you really feel the impact of the knuckle. In my eyes I was a tough so-and-so but this was a real eye-opener and I had to be clever to buy some time and let my head clear.

The crowd were on my back but I remember sticking my chin out and swearing through my gumshield. Just as I was starting to feel comfortable, Hunt floored me with a huge shot. I'd only been put down a couple of times in my previous fights in nightclubs, pub car parks, and the unlicensed game, but here I was on the deck seeing stars. I'd never been hit that clean before and if it had been a cartoon I would have had a couple of birds flying around my head.

There was no way I was getting stopped on my debut, though. That simply wasn't going to happen. I got to my feet slowly and for the next four rounds I just did all I could to hold on and waste time. I was running away, hitting him in the bollocks and getting warned by the referee, spitting my gumshield out so the timekeeper had to stop the clock. Anything to throw him off his rhythm.

Eventually, the final bell sounded and it felt like the biggest achievement of my life. I'd got through my first professional fight without getting knocked out and gone the full distance. The crowd were clearly annoyed that there was no brutal stoppage and I was still standing but their man was a comfortable winner. The announcer grabbed the microphone and the place went quiet.

'Your winner, ladies and gentlemen, Rob … Hunt.'

The score was 40-36 which meant I had lost every round. There was a little part of me that was gutted to be completely whitewashed. I thought I had nicked a round or two at least. I had become accustomed to winning fights on the street and in the unlicensed arena so it was a new feeling and one I didn't particularly like. But this was my job now – I was paid to lose.

'I'm going to have 100 fights,' I said to Carl as I climbed out of the ring.

'Fuck off,' he said, 'you've only just had one!' and laughed.

But I knew I would have more. A lot more. Because despite the insults, the fear, the pain, even the losing, I loved it. Absolutely loved it. This was me, Johnny Greaves. I felt alive for the first time in my life. I stuck a couple of bottles of lager under my jacket and walked out of that leisure centre like John Wayne.

7 July 2007

Fight 3:
Johnny Greaves v Jamie Cox
O2 Arena, London

I had done ok in my second fight on a small show at Dudley Town Hall and was starting to feel a little more at home in the professional game. Nonetheless, I did wonder if all my fights would be in the arse end of nowhere in front of one man and his dog. So, the setting for my third bout came as a welcome surprise – the O2 Arena in front of 20,000 people.

I was told that there would be a weigh-in the day before in front of the media, a press conference, live TV interviews, the works. This was what I had imagined when I turned professional. The trouble was my opponent was going to be a whole new level as well.

Jamie Cox had won a Commonwealth gold medal and was a knockout merchant as an amateur. Jamie sparked people out for fun. You might have seen him in more recent years fighting the likes of world super middleweight champion George Groves. He's become quite a name and gone on to fight at a weight a full two stone heavier than when he fought me, so that shows the natural size and strength of the man. I knew loads of boxers who wanted no piece of him but when I got the call from Frank Warren offering me more than double what I had earned in any fight to date, I didn't have to think twice.

Frank Warren was the main man in British boxing at the time, and still is now. He has been the biggest boxing promoter in the UK for near enough 40 years and is a very influential man in the sport. He's a real character too, all sharp suits and Bentley cars with personalised number plates. He represented lots of the boxers and would put on big shows every week. Warren had guided the careers of some the biggest names in boxing, representing guys like Nigel Benn, Joe Calzaghe, Ricky Hatton and Prince Naseem down the years, as well as Tyson Fury in more recent times. Who was I to be in his company and on one of his shows? Some bloke off a building site with his lunch money and a pack of fags in his back pocket. I had no business here.

The O2 itself was massive, the biggest arena I had ever seen. All the big stars play there. I'd been with Vicki to watch a couple of bands but never in a million years imagined myself fighting there. The rows of black seats went up as far as you could see, there were fancy corporate boxes all around, and there were lighting rigs and cameras everywhere you looked.

People were paying hundreds, maybe thousands of pounds to come and see me box.

Of course, that was far from the truth. I was just making up the numbers, with names like Amir Khan, Kevin Mitchell and Nicky Cook the headline acts that people were interested in. Nobody had even heard of me. I could wander through the arena and not a single person would have batted an eyelid, never mind asked for an autograph. The only person likely to recognise me was the woman whose bathroom I had tiled the previous week or maybe a copper who had cautioned me after a street fight!

I was asked to take part in a press conference for the first time and felt really self-conscious. All the boxers were sat on the stage with their names on little placards in front of them and ahead of us were 30 or 40 media people, all asking questions. I was sat amongst these established boxing names and I knew they had no idea who I was and didn't care what I had to say. It lasted about an hour and in that whole time only one question was directed at me. Someone asked me how I felt about fighting Jamie and what my hopes were for the fight.

'I fancy myself for the win,' I said.

There was a ripple of laughter among the knowing journalists and even some of the fighters. I wanted the ground to open up and swallow me but tried to style it out, swigging my water and giving Jamie a little look.

After that we had a face-to-face on the stage, up close and personal for the cameras. We stood inches apart and I threw a few insults at him to try to get a rise but he just smirked back, looking me up and down with disdain.

I should point out that I wasn't the most intimidating of physical specimens. I had my mum's build. I was only 5ft 8in tall and 10 stone, not the kind of frame to have people quaking in their boots. My face was more of a giveaway though, with a few lumps and scars around the eyes, and I had a crew cut and stubble.

I didn't mind being the underdog and I liked it when people underestimated me. Like at school when I was earning a reputation as one of the toughest kids in the area. People started talking about a lad called Terry who went to the school down the road. He was harder than me, they said. He would give me a good beating. I didn't even know what he looked like but people would tell me that he was looking for me, that he wanted to prove he was the toughest kid in Upton Park. One day I came home from school and this boy was waiting at my front door. He looked solid and strong, a couple of years older than me for sure.

'You John Greaves?' he asked.

I didn't need to answer. He walked over and made a play for me so we went at it on the pavement. I wasn't going to back down. It didn't matter to me if he was hard or not. If he was, then I would take all he could give me. But I wasn't going to be intimidated by him or anyone else. As it was, I had the better of it and he walked away knowing he had been well beaten. That was me. I never ever backed down from anybody.

My opponent at the O2 had a real pedigree and was a fighter who had been tipped for big things when he turned pro. If you don't know the difference between amateur and professional boxers it's quite simple – money. If you have talent in the amateurs, where you fight for nothing other than awards and recognition, then you turn pro and earn a few quid. Anthony Joshua would be the best example in recent years, having won Olympic gold as an amateur and then linking up with Eddie Hearn's Matchroom stable and becoming a huge global star.

If you've had a good amateur career it usually means you've been fighting from a very young age, are well-skilled and pretty intelligent in the ring. Jamie Cox ticked all those boxes and that wasn't good news for me, but I heard his pre-fight interview and he sounded quite respectful.

'I'm fighting a lad from East Ham and he's supposed to be quite durable, so I'm ready to go the full distance. He lost his first two pro fights on points so I expect him to be able to last the fight. I've been doing a lot of endurance training and sparring but we're cutting down on it now to save my energy for the fight.'

He was clearly taking things a bit more seriously than me. I'd been renovating some flats in Lewisham and having a couple of pints with my mates.

My brother Frank was with me and he looked so nervous in the dressing room before the fight. It can't be easy knowing your little brother is about to step into the ring with one of the most feared punchers in British boxing. Especially when you know that same little brother has done fuck all training and was in the pub the night before. I think the venue and occasion probably affected us both as well.

Barry McGuigan, the former featherweight world champion and BBC Sports Personality of the Year back in the 80s, was mooching about backstage. I was chuffed when he approached me before the fight.

'Who you boxing?' he asked.

'Jamie Cox,' I replied.

'Ohhhhh good luck son!' he said, and walked away chuckling to himself.

Now I was starting to get a little more worried but my mindset was simple: he can hit me with a house brick and I ain't going down. Not tonight. And there was even more motivation than normal. This was the night Mum came along to watch me for the first time. There was no way I was getting knocked out in front of her. It felt different having her there. I wasn't fighting for myself this time. I wanted to make her proud. To show her that I could look after myself.

As I sat in the dressing room, listening to the music blaring out in the main arena and the sound of people starting to take their seats, those thoughts went round in my head again.

'Show Mum that you're worth something, show her you are worth loving.'

I fought back the tears, putting a towel over my head and trying to sort myself out.

I spent what felt like an age backstage and it was horrible. You're with all the other fighters and you feel their nerves, see the fear in their eyes. It was always a relief when your name got called out.

As I made my way to the ring, I was desperate to find Mum in the audience, but the lights were blinding and the place was so big. I was squinting and trying to get my bearings. No sign of Mum. Then all of a sudden I caught her a few rows back. She looked beautiful. She was standing and cheering, shouting my name. Something in me shifted and I felt myself welling up again. Whatever I did tonight was for her. I blew her a kiss and climbed into the ring.

I bounced up and down on the red and white canvas, swaying back on to the ropes, practising getting out of the way of shots. Then my opponent was announced and the crowd came to life.

A lot of people were fancying Cox to go a long way in the game, maybe even fight for a world title, and they were making a lot of racket. I tried to stay in my bubble, hopping from one foot to the other, hitting the gloves into my own head as a show of toughness. I even gave Jamie a little glare as he walked past my corner and mouthed 'come on son' at him. He looked totally unfazed.

The bell went and Jamie walked straight across the ring and caught me with the biggest sledgehammer cross I'd ever been hit with. Fuck. I was down in the first round.

I could hear the crowd going crazy as I tried to get my bearings. I could just about make out the referee's voice:

'Five, six, seven …'

The only thing that makes you able to stand up in that situation is instinct. My heart would never let me stay down and my mind was telling me to get the fuck up and fight on.

I clambered to my feet at seven or eight, much to the annoyance of the home crowd.

'Fucking kill him, Jamie!'

'Knock his fucking head off.'

The Cox supporters were desperate for an early stoppage but it helped me in a way. There was no chance I was going to let these arseholes get what they wanted. I thought of Mum again. I couldn't see her, I couldn't see much to be honest. I was struggling to get my balance back and see straight, but in my mind's eye she was looking worried, upset, maybe disappointed.

My head started to clear a bit but I could feel the strength had gone out of my legs and I'd lost that ability to move and avoid punches. I drew on every childhood memory, every time I thought the punches would never stop.

I was desperate, absolutely desperate, for the final bell. I kept looking at the referee and timekeeper, almost urging them to finish the contest early. I was blowing out of my arsehole and a little bit of blood from a cut on my forehead was running into my eye, obscuring my vision and making it even harder to fight.

He threw his final combination and I covered up, doing my best to parry the shots on my gloves and arms, but even they were hurting badly from blocking so many punches. The final bell sounded and I gave Jamie the biggest hug I could muster, falling into his arms almost. I was grateful, relieved, proud, fucking exhausted.

'You're one tough cunt,' he whispered to me, and for the first time that day I raised a little smile. I marched across to where Mum was sitting and screamed out.

'I'm still fucking standing!'

She smiled back and blew me a kiss.

'Ladies and gentlemen, give your appreciation for Mr Johnny Greaves,' said the ring announcer.

I walked back through the crowd, beaten but defiant. I'd got in there with a big puncher on a huge arena show and made it to the final bell. If I could survive that I could survive anything. At least in the ring, anyway.

Chapter Seven

Tears of a Clown

10 December 2007

Fight 8

Johnny Greaves v Darren Hamilton
Holiday Inn, Peterborough

The money from the boxing should have made us better off as a family, but it didn't seem to make a lot of difference. Vicki and I both liked our designer clothes and would spend more than we should on shopping trips to Lakeside. I was also drinking too much and spending any spare cash on cocaine, so we invariably ended up skint. That had got worse since the arrival of little Teddy, who was now coming up to two years old. We already had a flat full of baby stuff – toys, prams, high chairs and goodness knows what else – so when Vicki announced she was pregnant again, we had no choice but to try to find a bigger place.

We had managed to get out of Manor Park about six months earlier, renting a flat above a shop on Hornchurch High Street. That had been a huge relief because Hornchurch was a decent place but now we were going to need more room and Vicki was keen to be nearer her mum in Chadwell Heath, so we moved into a three-bedroom council house in Becontree. It was a pretty rough area, all slate grey terraced housing and little parades of shops with groups of kids hanging about and up to no good, but compared to Manor Park it was like living in Hampstead Heath. The house was very old and tatty and needed a lot of work but at least it was ours.

Becoming a dad and having more financial commitments should have made me more responsible but I found daily life a struggle. Painting or labouring didn't exercise my brain much and it was always hard work for very little money. I couldn't ever see myself getting a better job and the constant grind made me feel depressed. I would spend most of the week looking forward to Friday or Saturday nights on the road. It was my chance to become someone else for a while. To escape.

I had fought a future world champion in my sixth fight and not disgraced myself so I was starting to believe I belonged as a professional boxer. Anthony 'Million Dollar' Crolla, had been an Amateur Boxing Association (ABA) champion, the highest accolade in the amateur game, when I fought him and still remains one of the proudest names on my record. He was very slick but his power didn't trouble me and, as it turned out, we had a nasty clash of heads and the fight had to be called off. That was as good as a victory in my eyes.

The way I saw it was that nobody had stopped me so far, and nobody ever would. I was getting cocky to the point of arrogance and it was only a matter of time before that caught up with me. I was going a bit too far with my ring persona and playing up to the crowd more and more, sticking my chin out, dancing, talking to people in the crowd. It was almost a circus act and the boxing purists weren't impressed.

In my eighth fight I faced a lad called Darren Hamilton on a show at the Holiday Inn in Peterborough, another of the glamour venues on the British boxing circuit! It was a small event with a couple of local fighters selling most of the tickets, with the ring set up in a conference room that you would usually see used for those boring business events. This was a world away from facing the likes of Jamie Cox or Anthony Crolla in big arenas so I was relaxed and determined to enjoy myself.

Hamilton was a really talented fighter. He was known as 'Ammo' because he could talk for England. He also had a really interesting background, having been brought up in Bristol and living on the streets for a while before finding boxing. I'd even read somewhere that he worked as a cleaner and lived in the broom cupboard when he was struggling to make ends meet. Anyway, he was a tough lad who had seen it all outside the ring and wasn't afraid to mix it. There was one fight where he had broken his nose in three places but boxed on until it was eventually stopped due to too much blood.

He wasn't a guy to take lightly but needless to say, I did. In my mind, I had fought guys on a different level and could take a few liberties with this bloke. He was throwing shots and I had my hands behind my back, bobbing and weaving, sticking my tongue out at him and the crowd. The referee, a guy called David Parris who was quite old-school, didn't like it and warned me a couple of times. He thought it was disrespectful and not in the spirit of boxing. I ignored him and carried on playing the fool, holding on, hitting my opponent up the bollocks, smiling and winking at the crowd.

The referee has a lot of power in boxing and most of the decisions during a fight are at his discretion. Well, after a couple of verbal warnings, Dave decided to stop the bout. He pulled me aside in the middle of the contest and waved his arms in my face to make it clear he had seen enough. I was stunned, as were the crowd. It was only my eighth fight but from what I had seen, referees understood the role of journeymen. They knew we were there to entertain. Well, not Dave. He said I wasn't defending myself and awarded the fight to Hamilton. I was fuming and started whipping the crowd up.

'Fifty quid to the first person who sings "the referee's a wanker",' I shouted out.

The crowd were in hysterics and a few chants started up. Dave was properly unimpressed and just walked out of the ring without looking at me. I half thought I might be called up by the board and banned for misconduct, but I heard nothing.

I did begin to wonder, though, if I needed to take things a bit more seriously because the BBBC, who hand out the licences each year which allow you to fight, kept quite a close watch on things. If they deemed that I was taking the piss or it was obvious that I had no intent to win, they might revoke my licence. I'd heard that if you lost four fights in a row they could call you in and ask to see a training diary – whatever that was – and talk to your coach to see if you were living the right life and showing the necessary dedication and ambition. That was a load of bollocks really and made no sense. If you fought too hard and won then you wouldn't get booked for any more shows. If you swung for the trees and got cut or knocked out then you couldn't fight for another 28 days. So what were you supposed to do? The answer was to LOOK like you were trying to win but be clever in the process. Slip and move, feint, throw little shots that were range-finders more than knockout punches, hold on, waste time. There was an art to this game and I was learning quickly what a cynical business it was.

23 February 2008

Fight 11

Johnny Greaves v Sergejs Rozakmens
Grove Leisure Centre, Newark

I had fought ten times and lost all of them. My friend and promoter Carl was still quite new to the promoting game and seemed a bit concerned. I was one of the first fighters he had signed to his stable on a proper contract and he was worried about the board and the possibility of them taking away my licence. My antics in the ring were not to everyone's taste and being thrown out against Darren Hamilton had got people talking. There were lots of other journeymen out there, including a guy called Peter Buckley, who eventually had 300 fights and once went 65 contests without a win, but a lot of those guys gave the impression of taking it seriously. I was treating fights like they were a joke.

So we had a chat and decided to try to organise a fight for me where I had at least a chance of winning.

The politics of boxing didn't make a lot of sense to me. The board knew how boxing worked and the job that we did as journeymen. They understood that my type of fighter made the promotions up and down the country run smoothly and the role we performed. Why did we need to be seen to be winning fights?

Either way, Carl was getting worried that they would start asking questions so lined me up with a fight against another journeyman of his called Sergejs Rozakmens. He was a Latvian who was living in Nottinghamshire and doing exactly the same job as me. We were both losing fighters but, for tonight, one of us needed to win to keep the authorities happy. Carl was effectively pitting two of his journeymen together in the hope that I might be able to get a win. Surely anyone with half a brain would see that? But fuck it, I wasn't going to say no and the prospect of actually winning a fight was pretty appealing after ten straight losses.

The fight took place at yet another leisure centre, this time in Newark. It is a little market town between

Nottingham and Lincoln where Carl had a gym and a load of local fighters would train with him. He would put on shows in the town or surrounding area and those lads would sell a bunch of tickets. These shows weren't on television and wouldn't have got much attention outside the local area but they were always well-supported. Carl was swanning around in a waistcoat and smart trousers, chatting to all the fighters and BBBC officials, making sure the event went smoothly. He was a cool customer was Carl, but he seemed anxious that my fight went to plan and we had a couple of chats about what I needed to do.

Rozakmens wasn't a big lad, about the same size as me, but very durable and tough. He had lost 21 of his 24 fights but he was simply playing the game and making a few extra quid like me. If he had wanted to win some of those fights, I'm damn sure he could have done. So I didn't really know if he was any good or not.

He had agreed to be the away fighter, so for the first time in my career I was introduced to the crowd last. Not that anyone really cared. We didn't have any fans between us and everyone had come to watch the headline fighters who they knew. I don't think too many of the punters had the first clue who either of us was but it didn't matter to me. It was a payday and the chance to tell friends and family I had actually won a fight, assuming things went to plan. I would skip the details about the circumstances and the fact my opponent was a journeyman himself. No need to spoil the moment.

I actually boxed well that night and in the very first round threw a peach of a left hand which dropped him to the canvas and, to my amazement, the referee stopped the fight. Whether Rozakmens had been told to stay down, didn't fancy it, or I genuinely stopped him, I'll never know. But my hand was held aloft for the first time and it felt good. The crowd cheered politely, I took the applause and wondered why it couldn't always be like this. How had I got myself into a world where losing was a habit? I didn't want to think about that tonight. I knew I had to savour this feeling because it would be a long time coming again. It would keep the board off my back for a few weeks but there were much harder nights to come.

17 March 2008

Fight 14
Stuart Green v Johnny Greaves
Radisson Hotel, Glasgow

I was now into my second year as a professional boxer and that win against Sergejs Rozakmens would continue to be very much a one-off. The vast majority of my fights were on the road, travelling alone with no trainer and no tactics, facing the fury of a pumped-up home crowd and their local hero. That would be followed by the inevitable loss, usually on points.

It was hard saying goodbye to Vicki and little Teddy each time. She was carrying our second child and I felt guilty for leaving them. She was already on her own most days when I was at work or training. It wasn't much of a life for either of us really. We were just surviving. If she was lonely, then I was too.

I did actually have a trainer. He was an ex-boxer by the name of Jason Rowland who had been the British and world light welterweight title holder. He trained a few fighters down at the Peacock Gym, so when I was applying for my licence we had a little chat and he said he was happy to show me the ropes. I wasn't inundated with offers and didn't know many people in the fight game so it was an easy decision to make. I had also watched Jason on TV and knew what a good fighter he was. I needed to use the expertise and experience of someone like him so we started working together.

There were two issues though – firstly, he was pretty busy with his other fighters and he probably didn't think I was going to make much of a career out of the sport. We would do sessions on the pads and he would give me some advice but I didn't feel like his priority. Why should I have been? But it would have been nice to feel a bit more valued maybe. The second issue was that Jason had been a terrific fighter. He wanted his boxers to be aggressive and show ambition and do the things that he had done. The trouble was that I wasn't capable of fighting at that level and, to be honest, the job of a journeyman is very different. He either didn't understand or didn't embrace that, but I found his tactics a bit strange. I would have loved to walk forward and throw shots but most of the guys I was facing were a lot better than me. This was mainly about survival.

I had been offered a fight in Scotland against a lad called Stuart Green and I didn't really fancy travelling all that way alone, but Jason was busy so I packed as usual and got the train up to Glasgow. That was a hell of a journey and took the best part of a day. We had to be there 24 hours before the fight for the weigh-in and that was likely to mean only one thing – a night of drinking. I sat in the hotel bar alone, miles from anywhere and anyone I knew, and felt pretty alone. A million thoughts raced through my head:

'Who was I doing this for?'

'Am I a terrible partner and father for leaving Vicki and Teddy?'

'Who will be there for me if I get knocked out?'

'How long can I keep doing this?'

The only way to stop the thoughts was to have a beer. And then a few more.

I would often wake with a hangover on the day of a fight, but by the start time, the adrenaline would kick in and I'd be ok. In fact, sometimes I would fight better after a beer or two.

The fight against Stuart Green was one of my best performances and I still look back and think I won. It was a really small show at a hotel by the river in Glasgow. There were only two other fights on the bill but it was clear that Green was the guy being backed by the promoter and needing a win. He had mainly fought against journeymen and lower-level fighters in his 17 bouts to date but had already suffered six defeats so I fancied myself to do ok.

He wasn't up to much really and I navigated the fight with ease, putting together nice combinations and then using my footwork to keep out of range whenever he launched attacks. His style just suited me and I grew in confidence as the fight went on. I was certain I'd won at least a round or two, despite the Scottish fans at ringside telling me how shit and ugly I was throughout the fight. I was fully expecting the referee to raise my hand at the end but the ring announcer read out the scorecards and somehow I had lost by a wide margin. It was a complete joke.

That was the night when my mentality really started to change. The penny dropped that no matter how well I fought, I wasn't going to be getting any decisions. These fights weren't really being scored fairly. The referees and judges understood who the paymasters were and they played the game. It happens in boxing all the time, even in big televised fights. Politics always plays a part and it can spoil the purity of the sport, while for the fighters who are on the wrong end of those decisions, it's heartbreaking.

Going into that fight, a part of me still believed that I could achieve something in the sport. That maybe my talent and ability might be rewarded here and there if I performed well. But that night in Glasgow, as I sat in a cab back to the hotel on my own, I realised that I was kidding myself. What was the point of having a go and being the best version of you if nobody was going to recognise or reward it? I decided to start playing by their rules. If I couldn't win then I would make my mark in other ways. I would fight dirty. You'd know you'd fought Johnny Greaves and you wouldn't forget the experience.

I travelled back down south the next day feeling a bit the worse for wear after a few more beers to drown my sorrows and make the seven-hour journey pass more quickly. My mood wasn't helped by Jason texting me and asking me to drop his money over on my way home. He hadn't even bothered to be there so why was he getting a percentage of my fee? Also, his tactics weren't helping me. If anything they were holding me back. I noticed he was there for the big shows but never the ones in the arse end of nowhere. I liked Jason and don't want to sound too harsh but he was the wrong guy for me. There are no hard feelings but shortly after that I decided to split with him. It wasn't working and I wanted my brother Frank around more. He had driven me to a few fights and was keen to be in my corner. He understood the game really well and always looked out for me. He promised to get his coaching licence and be a bigger part of my team on the road as soon as he could. It would be just like old times, Frank looking out for his little brother. Except now the stakes were a little bit higher.

Chapter Eight
Self-harming
14 June 2008

Fight 16
Johnny Greaves v Liam Walsh
York Hall, London

We were now less than a month away from having a second child and Vicki was still in and out of hospital with Ted. Every time he grew, they needed to operate again. It was really tough on Vicki and I was trying to support her as much as I could. I'd be working in the day, then travelling home late on the tube in my overalls covered in paint, and spending the evening doing up the spare room ready for the arrival of the new baby.

Despite feeling constantly knackered, I would have boxed three times a week if I could. God knows we needed the cash.

I would happily have had a punch-up with anyone but boxing is divided into weight categories so you don't have some big bruiser smashing seven bells out of a little bloke. Although, to be honest, in boxing if there's a pound note involved almost anything goes. The rules can be pretty strict in theory, but it all depends which official is looking at the scales and who is paying him. They will deny it but in small-hall boxing, money talks. If you're on the payroll you do as the boss says and the sport isn't governed well enough to prevent all kinds of stuff happening. I've seen all types of tricks being pulled: blokes standing on one leg, hopping on and off the scales, officials writing down the wrong weight to ensure the fight went ahead and everyone got paid. Don't kid yourselves about boxing being a gentlemen's sport, it's a long way from that.

The fighter's health isn't always prioritised in the way it should be, although the boxers often pay little attention to their own wellbeing. At the lower level there's a lot of blokes who just want to have a tear-up to impress their mates in the crowd and earn a few quid. If they weren't doing it in a professional way they would be doing it on the streets on a Saturday night and if that meant fighting a bigger guy for a bit more money then so be it. Certainly that was true in my case. I'd have fought King Kong for a few grand.

Anyway, I was always just on the weight or very near it. I was naturally small and could eat pretty much what I wanted without putting on an ounce, which I duly did most days. Pork belly was my favourite, washed down with a few lagers and a fag or three. I never once thought about my diet because I didn't need to.

Frank was driving me to fights now and getting more involved. He would always be doing his nut, shouting at me for being unprofessional or bringing along protein shakes for me to drink instead of coffee. His heart was in the right place but eating the right food before the fight wasn't going to make a hell of a lot of difference when I was shovelling crap down my neck the rest of the time.

For the fights against knockout merchants, I would smoke a lot more as well. It was just my way of calming myself down. My only concern was avoiding getting cut or knocked out, that was it. Then I'd be out fighting again the next week.

We were still training at the Peacock in Canning Town. Frankie and me would be down there a couple of times a week. He would be stood in the centre of the ring and preaching about the importance of training right while I did the bare minimum. He would watch me punching the bags or doing my exercises on the mat and be shaking his head.

I couldn't bring myself to take it that seriously because I didn't see what difference it would make. I was going to lose anyway, so why work harder? It didn't make sense to me. But Frank and I would have blazing rows in front of the other fighters and usually not speak for a day or two.

One particular week I'd been meant to fight Chas Symonds. Chas was a mate of mine and still is. I was more than game to fight him, despite the fact we knew each other pretty well. It was the usual deal – money in cash, don't win if you can help it. The weight was 10st 7lb and I was around that most of the time anyway, but on the Monday night, Chas pulled out with an injury. I was gutted as it was money down the drain.

I was consoling myself with a glass of something cold and a spliff at home when the phone rang. It was Carl offering me a fight on the following Friday at York Hall, just around the corner. The only problem was they wanted me to fight at 9st 6lb. That meant losing the best part of a stone in five days – not a chance.

I had another pint and thought about it a bit more. I needed the money. I always needed the money. I had no idea how I was going to do it but I called Carl back and accepted the job. Now I needed to come up with a plan to lose the weight. A couple of grand to fight Liam Walsh was too enticing but I wasn't really sure how to do it. I wasn't a massive eater and there was barely any fat on me as it was. The other issue was that I couldn't be too weight-drained or I'd have no strength and get smashed to pieces. Liam was a very, very good boxer who would go on to fight for a world title, so this was risky. My thinking was that he was smaller than me so there was no way he could knock me out. I'd just keep out of trouble and pick up the dough.

The next day I woke up and realised what a stupid fucking idea this was. I had four days now to shift a stone in weight and still be strong enough to fight a possible future world champion. I went down to the sports shop and bought a sweat-suit, which was not advised. They are like tracksuits made out of polyester that make you sweat buckets. The problem is that you aren't losing actual weight, just water.

It dehydrates you and that water has to be replaced if you're going to go in the ring and have a fight. I ran and trained in the sweat-suit for the first few days and could feel the weight dropping off me but I was already as weak as a kitten. After each run I would want to eat or drink but I couldn't, so I just sat there feeling like shit. I kept thinking of the two grand and walking into that arena in a big fight.

That week I would come home from a full day of work on the building site and eat next to nothing. One day all I had was an ice cube in a bowl. It was something to chew on at least.

I was absolutely dead. Gone. I could barely put one foot in front of the other. In my head I knew this was really dangerous but the fighter in me wouldn't allow me to pull out.

The night before, I wanted to carb-load and refuel ready for the fight but I knew I couldn't risk putting on even a pound in weight so I had another ice cube or two and sat it out. I got an early night and woke up the next day feeling so feeble I could barely get out of bed. Vicki had been watching this all week and keeping her thoughts to herself but now she finally cracked:

'John – this is fucking stupid, you can barely stand up,' she said, a look of real concern on her face.

'I'll be alright once I get some food down me,' I tried to convince her.

She shook her head and rounded up Ted before heading out. I don't think she could bear to be around me and I couldn't blame her.

In my mind this was just another situation to get through. It wasn't going to be easy but nothing was ever easy for me and if there was one thing I was good at then it was gritting my teeth and surviving. I just had to get to the weigh-in and then stuff my face as much as I could. I'd be ok after that.

I made my way to Bethnal Green on the tube but I couldn't even stand up. My bag felt heavy in my hands and it was all I could do to stay awake from the motion of the train. I managed to get to York Hall and had half an hour until the weigh-in. My body was giving up on me and I lay down on some seats at the back of the arena and tried to have a kip.

I was woken a short time later by a security guard who wanted to get the venue set up for the event. He recognised me from a few of my other fights at York Hall and asked me if I was ok. I shrugged:

'I will be once this fucking fight is out of the way,' I said, and sloped off.

Despite everything I had gone through that week, my worry was still being overweight and the fight getting called off. I peeled off my tracksuit and even my pants to make myself as light as possible. I could hardly bring myself to look down. The scales flickered around 9st 6lb and 9st 7lb then suddenly stopped on the right weight. I was too tired to even feel relieved. I'd lost 14lb in a week and was a dead man walking. I should have said something or pulled out but it wasn't my style. I was here now. I just had to get this done.

Having made the weight I had two hours until the fight to eat and drink as much as I could and try to regain some strength. This is another strange thing about boxing – you have to make the weigh-in, often the day before, and can then eat and put on as much as you like for the fight. So in some cases, fighters are climbing into the ring much, much bigger than their opponent. It's dangerous and stupid but some people don't care as there is too much money at stake.

I walked to a few shops round the corner on Bethnal Green High Street and stuffed my face with doughnuts, sandwiches and crisps for energy. It felt amazing to get some proper food down my neck but it was too late to save me. Your body takes much longer to replenish and get your energy back and although I felt a little more awake now, I could tell I was still a shadow of my usual self.

This was the worst I had ever felt before a fight. It was madness and I knew it. A death wish.

I sat in the changing room and couldn't even put my boots on. Part of me hoped someone would notice and pull me out of the fight but nobody was focused on me. They called my name and I walked slowly to the ring. The lights and noise made me feel dizzy. I had to bend to get through the ropes and my legs almost collapsed from under me. I felt like I was going to pass out. I tried to bounce around and shadow box but I had nothing. Liam was too wrapped up in his pre-fight routine to notice but I was going to be fodder for him, an easier night's work than he could have envisaged.

The referee pulled us together and told us to touch gloves. I couldn't lift my arms and the referee looked at me as if I was being awkward. For one of the first times in my life I was scared. Not scared of getting hurt but scared because I knew there was nothing I could do to stop the inevitable. I heard the bell sound and slowly came forward. It was all I could do to hold my hands up and try to defend myself.

Technically and skill-wise, Liam was very high up the list of guys I'd fought: accurate and quick. He looked a class act too, stocky and strong with a shaved head and wearing bright blue three-quarter-length shorts.

I didn't see any of his shots coming, never mind have the reflexes to get out of the way. By the end of the second round I knew I was fucked. I had the strength of a toddler. Worse than that, my brain wasn't working properly. My vision was blurred and I couldn't seem to get my body to do what my mind wanted.

In the last round he hit me with a combination, ending with a shot to the ribs, and I couldn't stand up a second longer. I didn't even want to. I just collapsed, exhausted and could feel someone shaking me. I just lay there, helpless. Even my usual sense of pride had left me. I couldn't muster anything. It was the scariest experience I ever had in the ring.

Afterwards, in the changing room Frank kept asking if I was ok. He was looking me in the eyes and holding my head in his hands.

'Yeh yeh yeh,' I kept saying.

But I really didn't feel well. My mind was playing tricks. It felt like my brain was bouncing in my head like a rubber ball and I was worried that if I went to bed I might not wake up.

That night I went home and cracked open a can of lager. Vicki and the kids were asleep and I couldn't even bring myself to turn the lights on. I sat in the sitting room, the light from the TV flickering away, and I slowly drifted off to sleep in the armchair. I think I dreamt about not waking up. And it felt good. I didn't really want to live anyway.

6 December 2008

Fight 23
Johnny Greaves v Ryan Walsh
Excel Arena, London

I was now a father of two after the arrival of Ruby that summer. She was six months old and a beautiful little thing. Teddy was already at nursery, still needing regular treatment but getting stronger by the day. I had so much to be grateful for: a lovely partner and two beautiful kids at home, but my world was black. I couldn't see the good in anything and felt hopeless. I didn't want to get out of bed or go to work. It felt like wherever I went, people were talking about me, that nobody liked me. Maybe Vicki and the kids felt that way too?

It was all I could do to leave the house, and when I did force myself, I would be paranoid. It felt like people were looking at me on the tube or talking about me in the street. What were they saying? I'd look back, stare at people, ask them what the fuck they were talking about. Getting home was a relief but then I'd have Vicki and the kids to cope with. All I wanted to do was have a drink and go to bed as soon as I could.

This feeling had followed me around like a shadow for a lot of my life. As a kid I don't think I analysed my moods so much. But now I noticed them much more. I would have the thrill and excitement of the fights followed by these bouts of really low moods. I often wondered what the point of life was. I would look around and struggle to see a reason to go on. I'd thought that way for as long as I could remember so it wasn't new. It was just a bit more worrying now. I had hoped I would grow older and do things, get a girlfriend, a wife maybe, have kids and a good job. Things would feel better then. But I had lots of those things now and a new career as a boxer, even a few quid in my back pocket, but still the thoughts followed me.

I was so down all the time. Spending my days working, drinking or just wanting to sleep, and it was driving Vicki round the bend. She had two young kids to look after, and didn't have the time or the energy to care for me as well. This wasn't what she had signed up for.

It felt so different to when we had met all those years earlier. I had only been 18 and working in the pie and mash shop. There was a card shop that opened next door and a girl called Claire worked there. I would occasionally pop over there during my lunch break and have a little flirt with the girls behind the counter. We got quite friendly and one Saturday morning I was putting spuds in the potato peeler when Claire got out of a car with another girl. She was small and blonde, very young, and I thought she was absolutely beautiful. I caught her eye and thought that I would get myself over to the card shop sharpish when my next tea break came around. It turned out the blonde girl was Claire's younger sister called Vicki, and only 15 years old. It seemed wrong to make a move when she was so young, so I decided to wait until she was 16 and then ask her out. She was very shy and not too sure what to make of this scruffy little kid with a shaved head who had been kicked out of school, but she agreed to a date, so I got thinking about where we could go, somewhere that would really impress her.

I remember speaking to Dad about it and he told me that him and the boys were going to Romford greyhound track that weekend and suggested I bring her along. It wasn't exactly a table for two at the Ritz but I didn't have much money and knew Dad would buy the drinks, so the dogs it was!

Vicki and I got the bus together, sitting side by side and talking awkwardly all the way. I was a bit nervous about Dad and what he might say in front of Vicki. He wasn't known for his tact at the best of times and after a few drinks you never knew what he might come out with, but we arrived and he was sat around in the bar with his pals, Roger and Lou.

Romford dogs wasn't the most glamorous place in the world but for a teenager it was quite exciting. The floodlights, the bell sounding when the hare was running, the fluorescent lights and long bar, and the chance to win a few quid. It was a proper working man's night out with punters smoking inside, the place packed with hard-core gamblers, loads of old East London men with their flat caps having a bet and a good drink-up.

The night consisted of Dad holding court, telling rude jokes, and me and Vicki sat laughing, more through embarrassment than anything else. Vicki didn't know what the fuck was going on. She was really nervous and probably wondering what the hell she had got herself into. She was young, so drinking to calm her nerves. We were both half-cut as we walked back to Chadwell Heath, hand in hand.

In my eyes she was just beautiful. Young, pretty, innocent and such a sweet girl. I was her first proper boyfriend and God only knows what her family thought of me. Some rough little shit from East Ham who was three years her senior, had been booted out of school and liked a tear-up. I remember meeting her dad for the first time and being really worried. Her family were all football fans and I made the mistake of saying I didn't like football. I think her old man was pretty dubious about my intentions and the age gap didn't help. She was still at school and I'm sure he felt very protective. I would have been the same. I had convinced myself that he didn't like me and was secretly hoping the relationship wouldn't work out.

Vicki's family lived in Chadwell Heath and I was in Upton Park. Chadwell Heath was more posh, although that wasn't saying much. It was near the West Ham training ground and had a golf range next door and the Moby Dick pub nearby that did a cracking carvery. That might not sound like a lot, but round here, it meant something.

Every time I was with her parents I felt intimidated and like I wasn't good enough for their daughter. I'd feel paranoid almost and the voices in my head would get louder and louder:

'They don't like you.'

'You aren't good enough for their daughter.'

'They think you're a loser.'

I probably didn't help myself. I would mask my insecurity by being cocky and bragging about my amateur boxing but it didn't seem to impress them and then I would become more self-conscious. It was a vicious cycle.

Her dad definitely had his reservations but I understood him feeling protective. That's how I felt towards Vicki when we were out. She would get a lot of attention from other men and I could be pretty possessive and jealous. There were a few times we went out and fellas would pinch her arse and eye her up and I would get into scraps. I tried to calm myself down as I didn't want people thinking I was a troublemaker, especially her family and friends, but it was almost impossible to contain my anger when it happened.

There was one incident where it really kicked off though, and ironically, it might have been the moment they started to accept me as part of the family.

We had gone to City Limits, a bowling alley in Chadwell Heath near her house. We all walked in and as we passed the bouncers, one of them looked at Vicki and said 'nice arse sweetheart'. I spun around and told him to fuck off, already spitting with rage and ready to go. Before I knew what was happening he walked towards me and grabbed me by the legs. One of his mates had pulled my arms behind my back and between them they were marching me to the car park. They threw me on the concrete and one spat in my face.

I was going to fucking kill him. He smirked at me, thinking that would be the end of it. But before he could turn away, I swung a big left hand and caught him right on the nose. He looked shocked for a minute and staggered back but didn't go down. Fuck. He composed himself and then he and all his bouncer mates set about me. Punches to the head and body, me curled up on the floor taking kicks to the stomach, back and head.

I'd been in some scrapes before but this was bad. Just as I was on the verge of blacking out, I heard footsteps and the shouts from Vicki's dad and brother. They had heard the noise from inside the venue and come running out, screaming at these blokes to get off me. But instead of defusing the situation, the whole thing escalated and turned into a full-on brawl between them and us. In broad daylight, in front of all these people who had taken their kids for an ice cream or a bit of shopping, it was absolute carnage. People were cowering or taking cover behind their cars. But things were about to get even worse.

There was a screech of brakes and a load of bouncers came pouring out of a minivan. The heavy mob had clearly called for reinforcements, the sneaky bastards. These lads jumped out of the van, faces contorted and armed with baseball bats. Absolute hell broke loose and I've no idea how we managed to hold our own or escape with our lives intact, but I'm proud to say that we gave as good as we got. That said, I was the worse for wear. I had bruises everywhere and my teeth had been punched through my bottom lip. The shirt was ripped off my back and what was left of it was soaked in blood.

For about two minutes I didn't know if I'd been stabbed or not, but the adrenaline was pumping so hard and I was just happy to be breathing at this point. I glanced round and Vicki's dad and brother weren't looking too special either. They picked themselves up off the floor, blood all over the concrete. We limped to the Moby Dick like it was the end of some old western movie and had a good old laugh about it over a load of booze. There was something funny about it despite the shit we had caused and the state we were in. We had never really clicked, not in my eyes anyway, but for now it felt like I belonged: that maybe I had got their respect by doing the only thing I was good at – fighting.

Those memories seemed a lifetime ago now. Vicki and me were different people, fighting in a different way.

Fighting to keep the relationship alive and to support two little kids. Vicki feeling the pressure of managing on her own, and me completely consumed by my inner demons.

I think she needed a break from me, or maybe we had had an argument, but I decided to go and stay at my mum's for the night. Mum spent the evening asking if me and Vicki were ok and wanted to have a proper chat but I wasn't in the mood. I went to bed feeling like shit. I should have been at home with my kids, like a proper dad. But here I was in the spare room of my mum's place and I couldn't get my brain to switch off. These dark thoughts kept coming and were keeping me awake. Voices telling me I was a loser, that I wasn't good enough, that I would never amount to anything.

I sat up and turned the light on. I wanted to make the voices go away but nothing worked. I needed to get out of the house, so I slipped on my hoodie and jeans and, quietly as I could, crept out of the back door and down the alleyway behind the flats next door.

It was cold and the only noise you could hear was from the busy A13 down the road. I stopped and looked around. It was too quiet and I needed to find some life, maybe a pub or late-night bar somewhere. Something to distract me from my own thoughts. But around here there was nothing. These were the real wastelands of East London. Barking was just an artery for the trucks and cabbies to get into town every morning and night. Nobody stopped here, there was no reason to.

I turned the corner and got that famous view of the London skyline from the east side of town, all lit up on the horizon. The busy road snaking round the bend and down the hill into the capital and a different world. It crossed my mind to head into London – it would be busy at least and full of life. But I couldn't do it.

My whole body just slumped on the ground, the pavement freezing on my arse. I just sat and watched the traffic for a while, feeling nothing, then came a growing anxiety. The noise was in my ears, the car engines constant. I noticed I was sobbing, shouting something.

The noise just got louder and louder in my head. I don't know why I did it, but suddenly I was standing up and walking towards the main road. There was a gap in the traffic and it all went quiet.

And then I sat. I sat down in the middle of the road and waited.

I closed my eyes and prayed for everything to stop. The noise, the thoughts in my head. There was no way any car or lorry would have had time to see me. It would be instant. I'd be gone. Maybe I wouldn't even feel it.

But nothing came. I blinked and opened my eyes and there were cars in the distance. I don't remember deciding to stand up but the next moment I was walking, falling on to the grass verge in tears again.

I didn't want to be here anymore. I wanted to be somewhere else but I wasn't even man enough to take my own life.

I was weak. A coward. Pathetic. Just like the boy who stood and watched his mum get punched and kicked. I was nothing.

I wandered back to the house, quietly grabbing a beer from the fridge and turning the TV on. The light was flickering against my face, the sound of sirens was coming from outside. I thought back to when I first started boxing. I was convinced that I would die in the ring. That I would be a hero. It would be a tragedy but almost perfect in a way. I could die with some pride. But Vicki said if I did that to her she would hate me, and that the kids would hate me for leaving her in that way. It felt harsh but that could be Vicki sometimes. She knew me and understood that boxing was like self-harm. I wanted to get hurt. So if I died it would be like a suicide, my choice rather than an unfortunate twist of fate, and she couldn't respect that. Even in death I was destined to be a failure.

I felt disgusted with myself as the alcohol started to work its way through my system, calming my anxiety. Then came the self-hatred. The voices in my head were different now. Asking me how I could even think of killing myself, how selfish I must be, how I couldn't really love my kids. I just kept drinking and slowly the voices quietened. At some point, I must have drifted off to sleep.

Mentally, I wasn't in the right state to be getting into a boxing ring but I would always tell myself we needed the money, that I was being a good partner and dad by fighting and improving our quality of life.

I was back home with Vicki and the kids and trying hard to get my head together but that loss to Liam Walsh and the way I felt afterwards had taken a lot out of me. It was the first time I had been stopped and anyone that had watched that fight would have been deeply worried. I had been a shell of myself and lots of members of the board, not to mention people I knew in the game, must have been concerned. I was embarrassed but consoled myself with the idea that he would never have stopped me had I been fighting at my usual weight.

That week I had no fights scheduled and was doing more manual work, trying to keep busy and not allow myself to be consumed with my thoughts. I was doing early mornings on the tube to some shithole in London with all my painting gear, then spending all day on my feet working before heading home for a few cans and an early night. Work was physically demanding and I didn't have the energy to go to the gym. What was the point if I wasn't fighting anyway? Frank was on at me to keep a routine and look after my body but I wasn't in the mood.

My only plan that week was to head to the Peacock on the Saturday morning for a sparring session. I had arranged a move about with a mate of mine, a young boxer called Ryan Taylor. He had a fight approaching and wanted to sharpen himself up. He could really bang, could Ryan. Even with big gloves on he whacked harder than a lot of kids I faced in the ring, so we just went at it. There were no trainers or anyone to keep an eye on us. I don't even think I wore a head-guard. They are important for absorbing some of the impact of punches when you are training. Why take big head shots in training that might shorten your career or risk brain damage? That was the sensible view. Mine was 'fuck it, I can take it, why not?'

I revelled in taking his biggest punches, so we traded blows for about 45 minutes. Neither of us took a backwards step, firing in shots to the body and head, both determined to outdo the other. Then, covered in sweat and feeling exhausted, we sat and had a good fry-up and a cup of tea. Lovely Saturday morning it was. I said goodbye to Ryan, got the tube back home and sat down with a couple of cans of lager in front of the TV.

I was just scanning the channels for something to watch when the phone went. It was Tunde Ajayi, a trainer and promoter who now works with world light heavyweight title challenger Anthony Yarde. I could see Vicki looking at me out of the corner of my eye as the conversation unfolded. I knew Tunde a little bit from the Peacock and he asked me what I was doing that night. I was fucked to be honest and the idea of an afternoon film and a nap was really appealing, but he told me there was £1,000 in cash on the table to fight that night at the Excel Arena on an Amir Khan undercard against Ryan Walsh. Ryan was the brother of Liam, the lad who had stopped me when I was too weak to fight, and was another very promising young boxer. It would be a big event too. I was planning on watching it on TV. Amir Khan had won Olympic gold and was the poster boy for a new generation of fighters, so this was a massive deal and there would be a huge crowd. The Excel wasn't that far from me, in fact it was almost opposite the Peacock Gym. Khan was the headline act but there was also Audley Harrison, another Olympian and a guy that Sky had invested a lot of money in, who was fighting Derek Chisora. I wasn't sure I had enough left in me to go and fight after the sparring that morning but the money was too tempting. I avoided Vicki's glare and agreed to take the fight.

I think the call came at about 2.15pm and by 6pm I was in the ring in front of about 15,000 people. I can't say I felt my best, and maybe the beer helped me loosen up, but I sailed through it. Ryan was decent but nothing I couldn't handle. In fact, it was one of the easiest grand I've ever earned.

The trouble was that bit by bit, fight by fight, I was asking my body to absorb too much punishment. I wasn't getting stopped so I could take some form of pride by surviving and enjoying the profits. But these fights were wearing me down. Deep down, I knew that, I could feel it. But on the surface I was full of bravado. I was disrespecting the game and my opponents, believing that any version of Johnny Greaves would be tough enough. So when the call came to fight another future world champion in the making in his own backyard, I didn't think twice.

Chapter Nine

Even When You Win, You Lose

2009

I WAS jobbing away as a journeyman during the first half of 2009, fighting at least every other weekend on the road, not that it got any easier. You would have the odd night against a prospect who was clearly more hype than substance. Those were the times when you could relax, have some fun and throw a few punches, knowing you were unlikely to get stopped or knocked out. I felt a bit better about myself and the job if I was competing and holding my own.

There were also some really hard nights. Lee Selby is probably the most talented fighter I've ever faced when you look at his record and what he went on to achieve. He would become a very good British and world title holder, winning the IBF featherweight belt and defending it for three years, as well as having big headline-making fights against names like Josh Warrington, Ricky Burns and George Kambosos Junior. I faced him on a really hostile show in Newport, Wales, which was another level to any kind of crowd I had fought in front of. Pure hatred. Selby was another who would knock me down but couldn't knock me out.

Then there was Gary Sykes, Tyrone Nurse and Gavin Tait. They were all really good operators who would go on to compete at British and European title level. None of those guys could stop me either and, while I took immense pride in finishing on my feet, these fights were putting serious miles on my clock.

Frank was learning the ropes at this point, training me during the week and being super keen about diet and tactics – most of which I ignored – but he still didn't have his trainer's licence so wouldn't be able to be in my corner during fights. That is where your main trainer would normally be, shouting instructions during the fight and dishing out advice between rounds. Frank couldn't do that yet so just drove me to the venues and wrapped my hands, as well as offering little pearls of wisdom here and there.

Losing every week was starting to grind me down. Then out of nowhere came an opportunity to get the win I had been craving. There was a posh dinner show taking place at the swanky Jumeirah Carlton Tower in Knightsbridge and I'd been offered a fight against another journeyman called Ali Wyatt.

Now I knew Ali and he was a tough kid, but this was a bloke I could beat. Because it was a fancy dinner show for people with more money than sense, the boxing was more for background entertainment than for connoisseurs of the sport. That meant they just wanted two fighters who were relatively cheap and fancied a punch-up and I was happy to oblige. There was no home and away fighter, nobody had sold any tickets, no pressure from a promoter to throw the fight. This was exactly what I had been hoping for.

As much as I was proud of taking these fights at short notice against good fighters and holding my own, never being knocked out or stopped, it wasn't much fun telling the boys in the pub I'd lost every week. They didn't really understand. I was the only journeyman boxer they knew. I think deep down they thought if I was any good, I would win. Well now I had a chance to do just that.

Frank was still a part-time black cab driver at that point, which was handy as he could park pretty much anywhere in London and he didn't charge me for the ride. The journey into town was spent the usual way with Frank banging on about technical stuff, tactics for the fight and how I needed to fight smart. I was sat in the back having a fag out of the window and ignoring him. I wasn't listening because I had already decided in my mind that I was having a go tonight and no mistake. I didn't often get the chance to have some ambition and try to get the win so I was going to go out on my shield and we would deal with the consequences later.

I had a secret weapon in my corner that night as well. Jimmy Tibbs, a legendary trainer who had once fought on the undercard of Muhammad Ali against Henry Cooper, and been a very good fighter before going off the rails and ending up in prison. On his release he had reinvented himself as a brilliant trainer to the likes of Nigel Benn, Michael

Watson, Billy Joe Saunders and hundreds of others. He was a boxing genius with a reputation that went before him and somehow he had agreed to be with me for this fight. There was a bit of a family connection, which helped. He was an old friend of my dad's from Canning Town and a Peacock Gym regular, so we were often in each other's company, but I didn't think he would have any interest in doing my corner. I was a loser, after all.

I needed the help because I'd stopped working with Jason, and Frank wasn't quite ready to take over, so Jimmy agreed to step in for one night only. I felt incredibly honoured and lapped up every word he said. Usually I thought I knew best, but this was Jimmy Tibbs, master tactician and motivator. If I couldn't win with him in my corner I never would. He was real old school was Jimmy, a big thick-set bloke with a real presence. He had thick grey hair and spoke in a proper cockney accent. He had one of those deep voices with a real authority. I knew he would get me properly fired up and ready.

We got to the hotel and the venue was another big conference room with a boxing ring in the middle and smart tables around the outside. All the fighters had to get changed in one big room next door so I could look across and see my opponent as he prepared. He was there with his manager Chris Sanigar, who was a well-known character in boxing circles with a thick West Country accent. I could see Wyatt had the same intensity as me and was probably thinking the same thing – that this was going to be his best chance for a win. He had lost his last six fights so would be keen to stop the rot but I really fancied myself, especially with Jimmy in my corner. He just kept whispering in my ear about how good I was, how I was going to knock him out, how I was going to make my family and friends proud. He was brilliant, Jimmy, and I felt unbeatable with him alongside me. The reality was that I was very beatable indeed but not by Ali Wyatt, and not tonight.

I was sharp, used my feet really well, flicked out the jab and stepped in behind it with hurtful shots when I could see he was on the back foot. I was winning the rounds, not by a lot but I was doing enough work. He was stepping forward and throwing a lot of punches but most were missing or hitting the gloves. In the final round, I knew I just had to avoid getting stopped and the win was mine for the taking. I kept out of the way, mixing it up with body shots and fighting in close where I needed to, holding and draining him of energy.

We were both spent and although I could see how much he wanted it, the look in his eyes told me he knew he hadn't done enough. This was going to be an unusual feeling and one that I had only experienced once before, on a show where I knew I was meant to win. This was different. It was a legitimate 50:50 fight and I was pretty sure I would be victorious.

The referee moved towards me and raised my arm aloft. The crowd were only half-interested and gave a gentle round of applause but I didn't care. Jimmy smiled at me:

'Fucking proud of you, son,' he said.

Frank gave me a big hug and told me how well I had fought. I felt a million dollars. I rang Mum and Dad and told them the news. Nobody could quite believe it.

'You won? How come? Who was the other guy?' came the responses.

I was looking forward to a Sunday down at the working men's club with Dad and his pals. In my mind, I was finally going to get some credit. People were going to realise that I was capable of winning if given half a chance. The piss-taking would stop.

But it didn't turn out like that at all. People either weren't very interested or were asking stupid questions like, 'Are you sure the other lad was trying to win?' or 'How bad was the other fella then John?', then everyone would have a good laugh. I laughed along and slowly got pissed but inside it was killing me. Why couldn't anyone give me some praise? Why was I always the loser, even when I won?

I kept my mouth shut and wondered what was the point of it all. Who was I doing this for? I didn't need to answer that because I already knew. This was all to make myself feel better. But win or lose, I never really did. Not for long anyway.

21 August 2009

Fight 39

Johnny Greaves v Gavin Rees
Newport Centre, Newport

The call to fight Gavin Rees made me uneasy for two reasons. Firstly, and unusually, I had not only heard of him but actually watched him on TV and rated him highly. Gavin had won 27 straight fights on his way to becoming world title holder before losing his belts last time out against Andriy Kotelnik. It had been a huge show at the Cardiff Arena in front of thousands of fans. He was a big name in Wales and boxing in general, was Gavin. I had watched him many times. Quick, sharp, solid, a really good fighter. And now here he was coming off the back of his first defeat and the pain of losing his belts and who was standing in his way, ready to take all that angst and aggression and vitriol? Me.

The second reason I felt a bit unsteady was the thought of heading back to Wales. I hadn't endeared myself to the Newport boxing crowd after the Selby fight, when I gave them a mouthful at the end and had to be ushered out of the back door to make my escape. This was the same venue and most likely the same fans. They weren't going to forget the skinny little twat from East London. No chance.

Rees's promoters had a problem as the two previous opponents they had lined up had pulled out. They had feigned injury most likely, but more often than not it meant a fighter didn't really fancy the job if he pulled out that late in the day. I didn't think twice about taking the fight, despite the apprehension. It was good money and the chance to test myself against a quality fighter. A little part of me always believed I could cause an upset but, if not, I would leave my mark. Make a name for myself. That's how I saw it.

Frank was worried because he knew how good Rees was. We all did. He was a busy fighter more than a knockout artist but those guys were clever and could wear you down. Still, facing those Welsh supporters was as daunting, if not more so. They really seemed to hate me and I wondered if it stretched back to my unlicensed days when I fought the Welsh champion at the Cardiff Coal Exchange and Alan Mortlock thought it would be a good idea to wrap me in a St George's flag. To say they wanted to kill me was an understatement and I'm not sure how I got out of there alive. That on top of me acting like a big man after the Selby fight meant this was going to be an uncomfortable night.

I made the familiar trip across London on the underground and then got the train from Paddington with a few cans of lager. I would need those to make the journey bearable. I still had no trainer, although Carl had another fighter on the show and said he would meet me there. So I travelled alone and had that horrible feeling in the pit of my stomach. Rees was going to be one of the best fighters I had ever faced, no question, and it was one of the few times I did give some thought to how I could keep him off me for six rounds. A loss was fine, I was used to those. I just needed to avoid a stoppage or knockout.

I met Carl at Newport station and reacquainted myself with the delights of the place. It made Canning Town look like Las Vegas. Most of the women had teeth missing, never mind the men, and for once I just wanted to get to the venue. Fighting was going to be more enjoyable than spending a few hours in downtown Newport.

Joe Calzaghe, the brilliant former super middleweight world champion and friend of Gavin Rees, was there so we had a chat. He was really polite but I could tell he thought I was a bit mad to be taking on someone of Gavin's class. He was probably right but the call had only come the night before and I wasn't in a position to say no.

Rees was a little bald bloke, stocky and hunched. He came flying out of his corner at the first bell, ready to have a real go. He was the first world champion I'd boxed and the class was obvious immediately. He caught me with some lightning fast combinations early on and it triggered something in me. Maybe I knew I couldn't survive this one with the usual tactics but I started to swing punches with real venom. I would have to hurt this bloke to slow him down. Put a dent in him.

The crowd were loving it, all fired up and so close to the ring you almost felt like they might step through the ropes and give you a whack themselves. They could tell I was a lamb to the slaughter. Each punch that landed brought cheers and he was making me miss every time I tried to counter. I was game though and the crowd appreciated that. I threw a six- or seven-punch combination, desperate to get him off me, but it took all my energy and he would just pivot and catch me with shots that I didn't see coming.

By the third round my left eye was closed and my vision was badly affected. It was hard enough with two eyes, never mind one. Carl was in my corner and kept asking me if I wanted to carry on. I could see the concern on his face. He had boxed at this level and knew when a fighter was in danger.

At the end of the fifth round, with no sign of Rees slowing up and my face heavily marked, he told me he was pulling me out of the fight. He gave me a big hug and held my head in his hands.

'I don't want to see you take any more punishment, John. Come on, let's go home.'

Any other time I would have complained and kicked off, desperate to prove him wrong. But I was done. Spent. I knew he was right.

Carl paid me the most money I ever earned that night but I think I was worth every penny. I sat on the train back with a few cans and a couple of grand in notes stuffed in my back pocket.

My eyes were closing with the swelling and I had bruises and cuts all over my face. I got a few looks from people sat nearby. I don't suppose many of them knew I had shared a ring with a recent world champion that night. That should have given me a sense of pride but being pulled out of the fight by Carl didn't sit easily with me. I was Johnny Greaves, the survivor. I always made it to the final bell, didn't I? Well now there were doubts. Questions in my mind. Yes, I was tough. I had proved that time after time. Gavin Rees was a world-class opponent, too. That counted for something, surely? My mind wouldn't rest so I drowned out the noise with lager and fell asleep before the train had even left Wales.

Chapter Ten

The Drugs Don't Work

24 October 2009

Fight 41

Oisin Fagan v Johnny Greaves
National Stadium, Dublin

When I first stepped into the professional arena, I believed I was tough. I believed that nobody could stop me. But fight by fight, those ideas were being challenged and broken down. Once you know that you can be hurt, dropped and knocked out, you're never quite the same fighter.

On the outside I was still talking a good game, but I didn't really believe any of those things any more.

Drink and drugs had always been present in my life, but now they became a regular part of my pre-fight preparation. It helped to shut out the fear and quietened the thoughts and worries that I shouldn't be doing this anymore. It also gave me an excuse or maybe a reason to fail. If I was abusing myself then the defeats weren't real. I could tell myself that a clean version of Johnny Greaves would have been able to cope.

The fight against Oisin Fagan at the National Stadium in Ireland was the start of a major spiral for me. At the time I was offered the fight, I still had a few grams of coke knocking about and decided that rather than leave it at home for Vicki to discover, I was better off taking it with me and maybe even using it to settle a few of the nerves.

I was meeting Carl at the airport but had already decided that he probably wouldn't approve, so made my way to the toilet before checking in. I sat down in one of the cubicles and got out the gear. I had a little look around for a camera just in case and then got out the sticky tape that I'd brought from home. I pulled down my tracksuit bottoms and boxer shorts and proceeded to tape the bags of coke to my bollocks. They had to be tight enough that they wouldn't stick out or fall off but also not so tight that it would rip all the hairs off my ball sack. This was not an easy operation but after a few attempts, I was happy that they didn't look too prominent and wouldn't be felt by any customs officer having a rummage around.

As luck would have it, I sailed through customs without attracting any attention. This was surprising because normally a little bald bloke covered in cuts and bruises arouses some suspicion. If there was a profile of someone who was likely to be carrying cocaine on a flight to Ireland from London, then I must have been it.

I was feeling pretty pleased with myself and decided to have a cheeky bag on the plane. As soon as we were airborne, I headed for the toilet and emptied the cocaine on to the top of the toilet lid. One more check that the door was locked and then, putting a finger over one of my nostrils, I took a big sniff. I stood up too quickly and got a head rush, so steadied myself and then dabbed what was left of the gear and rubbed it into my gums for a last little hit. I had a final check in the mirror to make sure there was nothing left on my nose, then headed back to my seat and ordered a beer. Carl was sat at the front of the plane and had no idea one of his fighters was doing that before a match. He was a good man, Carl, a sensible man who cared about his boxers and especially their safety. There was no way he would have let me get away with that and I felt bad that I was doing it behind his back. It felt like cheating on someone you cared about. That said, once the first few grams were in my bloodstream, there wasn't much I cared about besides myself.

I went out with Carl for a bite to eat and we talked about the fight. He knew I didn't want to pore over every little detail but I had to look like I was vaguely interested. He was telling me about Fagan's amateur record, his powerful right hand over the top, how he would come out aggressively and not to be sucked in by the atmosphere. He meant well and I should have listened but I'd been here so many times before. I told Carl I was going up to my room to relax and he gave me half a smile.

'Look after yourself, John. Be ready, he's a tough kid.'

I shrugged and decided in that moment that maybe I would try and behave myself. This was a big show and I still had my pride. I didn't want to get flattened in front of half of Ireland so, after sorting out my kit for the next day, I lay on the bed for a bit and watched TV. There wasn't much to do and I was bored shitless after about half an hour. I called home and spoke to Vicki and the kids, telling them I was getting an early night. I put the phone down and looked at the rest of the wraps of cocaine on the bedside table. I decided to have just a little tester, nothing more, but that was a huge mistake. I was buzzing now and full of energy, needing a smoke and a drink. I dug out my trusty shower cap, a must for all away trips, and stretched it over the smoke alarm to ensure it wouldn't go off when I had a fag. Then I called down to reception and ordered two pints of strong lager.

Now the night was rocking. The hours started to roll into one and I really can't remember how or what the fuck I was doing, but the next thing I knew I looked at the clock and it was 6am. SIX! Fucking hell. I was fighting that day. I was three grams light and seriously off my tits but rather than knocking it on the head and getting some kip, I decided I might as well finish what I'd started.

Over the next half an hour, as the sun came up over Dublin, I finished the last of my fags and snorted the final gram of coke. But I was so far gone that I couldn't get any more high or any more pissed. Nothing was having an impact and my mind began to jump. I could hear voices in my head telling me what a cunt I was, how I had let Carl down, how disappointed Vicki and the kids would be in me, that I would be knocked out and embarrassed in front of all those people. I just lay there consumed by hatred for myself, on the verge of tears.

I'd agreed to a medical before the fight, which was unusual but something the Irish organisers insisted on. I was only three or four hours away from having all kinds of machines wired to me. How the hell was I going to get through that? Was there a drugs test? Should I just tell Carl that I felt sick and pull out of the fight?

I desperately needed to sleep, even just for a few hours, but I was wide awake from the cocaine. My eyes were like saucers and my mind was racing. I was thinking of possibilities, excuses and repercussions. Maybe the board would find out and take away my licence. Carl might drop me as well. I'd be fucked.

I tried as hard as I could to get up and pull myself together. I was still as high as a kite but at the same time utterly exhausted. I showered and got changed, deciding that I would just blag it as best I could. I was getting good at that.

I managed to meet Carl and told him I was feeling nervous. My hands were shaking and I couldn't keep still, the cocaine still working its way through my system. We got a cab to the medical facility and I sat next to Carl, fidgeting and chatting away.

We arrived and, to my horror, there were all sorts of tests lined up for me. The doctor told me they would be looking at my heart rate and needed me to work up a sweat. Fuck. Now I was shitting it. There was no way I could run, not a chance. I could barely stand up. I had forgotten to bring any training gear so was forced to strip down to my boxers. They put me on a running machine and began to increase the pace. It was absolute torture.

After five minutes of jogging I thought I was going to have a coronary. I was sweating so much, breathing hard like I had completed a marathon. The officials were looking at me with concerned faces.

Eventually it stopped and I jumped off, almost falling to the floor with exhaustion. This was it, the end of the road. The medics looked at each other and compared numbers. There was quite a long wait as they discussed their findings. They were probably all in shock and wondering how a professional sportsman could have survived so long with such a lack of basic fitness. But then the main bloke looked at me and smiled:

'All good Mr Greaves, fit and well. We will see you tonight.'

I had passed somehow. I felt a mixture of relief and anxiety. I was pleased nobody had discovered my coke habit but now I actually had to fight in a few hours' time.

The drugs were wearing off by the time I got back to the hotel just after lunchtime but my body was broken and my mind exhausted. I managed to get my head down for some kip and was out like a light as soon as my head hit the pillow.

I managed a couple of hours' sleep but it was nowhere near enough. The alarm went off and I reluctantly got my stuff together and met Carl down in the foyer. I couldn't really look anyone in the eye, a combination of tiredness and shame sweeping over me. I was now feeling really paranoid as well, a come-down from the coke. I was worried about everything – my own health, people looking at me strangely, fears about the fight.

We got to the venue and I found my way to the changing room. Slowly the buzz of the event was taking hold. I could hear music blasting out in the arena, the Black Eyed Peas singing 'I gotta feeling, that tonight's gonna be a good night'. Something in me lifted as I listened to that and watched people filing into the venue.

My blood started pumping and I went into fight mode. I was here now, this was what I did. When Johnny Greaves was against the ropes he came out swinging. If I had to go down all guns blazing then so be it. This would be my time. And if I died, then I died. There would be some real honour in that.

I was introduced first, as always, and was ready to fight when an announcement came that there would be a hold-up of five to ten minutes. Fagan needed more time, apparently. It was a piss-take. I was warmed up and ready to fight. This was just an excuse to raise the drama and keep me waiting. Carl was pissed off and suggested we go back to the dressing room for a while and play them at their own game.

'Fuck that, I'm gonna stand here and put on a show,' I said.

So I took to the centre of the ring and started shouting and screaming, doing the Ali shuffle, dancing around to boos and jeers from the crowd. This was my moment and they could all fuck off. If Fagan wanted to take his time then I was going to steal his thunder. This was my stage now.

A few hours earlier I had wondered how I would get to this moment, but now I was pumped up. I was so switched on it was crazy. He could take as long as he wanted, I was going to keep building myself up and then take out all my anger on him when he decided to appear.

Eventually his name was called and the crowd went insane. The lights dimmed and a spotlight found him dancing and bobbing on the spot, looking primed and ready. He was a real warhorse. In his last fight, he had taken Amir Khan into the mid to late rounds despite suffering a broken ankle in the first.

The Irish crowd were so worked up and desperate for a big knockout but that night I boxed out of my skin. It was like a decent fighter had taken control of my body. I was using every trick in the book to keep him guessing. I noticed he was coming in low with his head down, so I started throwing the bolo punch. That is when the arm swings all the way round in a big circle and is brought up into an uppercut. Bosh. Success. Again and again it was finding its home. Oisin was one tough, tough bastard but I'm sure he was feeling it. The fight was scheduled for six rounds and after the night before, fighting at this pace, I had no business going past one.

It turned into probably my best showing to date. I remember thinking I had won at least a few of the rounds. Of course, when the scores were announced I'd only been given a share of three of the rounds and lost the other three. Still, after everything I had shoved up my nose the previous day, all the drugs and booze, this was the equivalent of a win in my eyes. The trouble was it gave me a confidence that I could abuse myself and still get in that ring.

I started to think that maybe a pissed-up, coked-up Johnny had a better chance. And it was more fun, too.

7 August 2010

Fight 53

Johnny Greaves v Gavin Prunty
City West Hotel, Dublin

I was spiralling out of control but very few, if any, people around me knew how bad things were. I was taking bigger and bigger risks, putting myself in the line of fire when under the influence of booze or drugs, barely able to defend myself properly against professional fighting men.

I knew deep down that sooner or later it would come to a head. It had to. Either the board would find out, and ban me, or I'd be brutally knocked out and get the wake-up call I needed. Or maybe even worse. It would be suicide by a different name.

The one person who had always known me and understood me better than anyone else was Frank. If there was one person who could get me to see sense it was him and, thankfully, he had now gained his trainer's licence and was going to be coming with me to fights and be in my corner. Whether he was motivated by a need to look after his little brother or he just loved the fight game, I wasn't quite sure.

I had got used to being a lone wolf. Travelling to shows on my own, paying one of the other trainers to be in my corner and throw some water on my face at the end of each round, thinking my way through the fights without any guidance.

A lot of other boxers thought I was mad. They would come with a trainer and their entourage, going through an extensive pre-fight routine, talking tactics between rounds and all that stuff. They would often look over and see me getting ready alone, taping my own hands, putting on the gloves, punching the wall to get the adrenaline flowing. They would seem bemused and ask where my team was. I would just tell them I didn't have a team and didn't want one. Then I'd blag it and offer 20 or 30 quid to one of the trainers or cuts men who was knocking around and ask them to be in my corner. They were usually happy to oblige. It wasn't ideal but I'd gotten used to it and it did mean I could do whatever I wanted, and by that I mean smoke, drink and eat shit. There was nobody to tell me any different and I enjoyed the freedom.

But Frank was now going to be by my side, just like the good old days as kids in William Worley Close. We decided he would drive me to fights, usually in his black cab, which was odd as there was no front passenger seat so I'd have to sit in the back like a paying customer and we had to talk through the intercom system. He probably felt like he was chauffeuring me around but I was uncomfortable as fuck on those hard seats and when you're driving four or five hours to a fight it's not ideal preparation.

It was far from perfect but still nice to have some companionship and Frank was excited to start training in the professional ranks. He had loved boxing all his life and considered himself a bit of an expert. Now he was a fully fledged trainer, with ambitions of getting more fighters on board and building a stable, so he was really stepping into the role. He had all his lotions and potions, tape for my hands, bottles of adrenaline and swabs in case I got cut. He looked like a doctor carrying his case filled with things for every eventuality. But it was good to have him there. It made me feel like he cared and someone had my back.

Frank knew that I was getting badly advised, that I was taking more punishment than I needed to. He was also well aware of my mood swings and depression, and the fact that I wasn't helping myself.

He was a very good thinker about the fight game and knew a lot more about other boxers than me. When an opponent was lined up, Frank would either know them straight away and start talking about their strengths and weaknesses, or he would sit and do his research, watching tapes and devising a game plan for the fight. It was never about winning – Frank knew the score and understood how boxing worked. It was about avoiding the punches and staying safe. The trouble was that he hadn't accounted for my pride and love of a scrap, something that would frustrate the hell out of him as I often turned a blind eye to all his well-thought-out plans.

I did think I had a better chance of reaching my target of 100 fights under Frank. My problem was that I fought on emotion rather than using my brain. If I was in a good head-space then I could listen and taken on instructions. If I felt crap then it was all out the window and I just wanted to fight. There was no talking to me. In those times I liked being hit. I wanted it, like a form of self-harm. That's why I would drink the night before a fight. Feeling hungover and not being able to properly defend yourself is scary. It forces you to come alive. It was a strange combination really, a part of me wanting to get hurt or even die in the ring, but then my survival instincts kicking in and me throwing punches back. I thought a lot about suicide but could never seem to go through with it, so this seemed a more natural way to kill myself. It wouldn't be me landing the blows but my lack of self-care. Putting myself in the ring in that kind of condition, that was in my control. I was hoping things would go badly wrong and was doing all I could to make that happen. I didn't care about the outcome, I wasn't scared of that. But something within me would fire up when I was really hurt or in danger and I'd grit my teeth and find a way to cling on.

I had been training a bit between fights but not with much enthusiasm. I would head to the Peacock after work, covered in paint and still wearing my overalls. I liked it once I was there but it was a real slog on winter nights to drag my arse to the gym after a full day of grafting. Jobs came and went but they were nearly always physically demanding. I couldn't be too picky seeing as I didn't have any qualifications and had been kicked out of school. More often than not I would be doing painting jobs but I'd usually fall out with someone before too long and have to find something else. I even drove a forklift truck for a while but got fired after driving it straight into the front offices of the company I was working for. I got my coat and left without even asking the boss if I still had a job.

So by the time I got to the gym I had usually been up for about 12 hours and didn't have much energy left. I would hit the bag, do a bit of shadow boxing, maybe the odd spar with a couple of lads if they were around. I preferred fighting to training so sparring was always more appealing. I'd always tell myself to go easy, but as soon as I got hit it became competitive and I would start trading and taking more punches than was healthy.

In terms of tactics, I didn't have any. I just made it up on the night depending on how I felt. I just preferred to trust my instincts, although to be brutally honest, my instincts had never been that trustworthy and usually got me in trouble. But because my lifestyle was so up and down, my mood was unstable. Sometimes the bell would go and I'd feel on it, sharp and strong. Other nights there was nothing there and mentally and physically I wasn't at the races. Maybe I hadn't trained that week or I'd hammered the booze and weed. Perhaps I had had an argument with Vicki or home life was getting me down. Then I would just have a tear-up. The more shit I felt, the more risks I took in the ring.

If people in the crowd laughed at my record or shouted abuse, it only fired me up. It was ok for me to think I was a useless cunt but nobody else was allowed to have that opinion and certainly not say it to my face. My favourite thing was to have a beer afterwards in the bar with the same fans who had been giving me dog's abuse. They would buy me pints and tell me what a hard bastard I was and how much respect they had for me. Then they would laugh at the stories of my lifestyle – the painting job, the lack of training, travelling alone to fights. They couldn't believe it, and I probably hammed it up a bit for my audience. I would have a few beers and a smoke on the way home and feel a bit better about myself.

Now when Frankie came on board properly, he wanted to change everything. Training was more focused and he wanted to work on things that would help me during a fight. He took it very seriously and acted like a proper trainer, barking out instructions and putting together a schedule to get me fitter but we were like chalk and cheese. He ate salads and drank four litres of water a day, I was on the weed and kebabs. He was the purist who wanted me to study tapes of my opponents and stay safe. I was the anarchist who did things my way and enjoyed the pain.

So it wasn't exactly a match made in heaven but if he could make this game even five per cent easier, then it would be worth it. The trouble was, because of his job and other commitments, he couldn't always be there or would sometimes have to join me on the day of a fight. That wasn't a massive problem in theory, but it meant that I was on my own the night before some fights and my self-control wasn't the best. Frank knew he couldn't trust me but there was nothing he could do about it. He would only get ten per cent of my purse to be in my corner during a fight which would work out at around a hundred quid at most. He wasn't going to be earning enough to give up his day job so we had to make do.

His first fight in my corner was against a guy called Gavin Prunty over in Ireland. I had been followed by a film crew for a couple of fights leading up to that trip. A documentary maker called Michael Mosley was making something for the BBC on the wonders of the human body. Why on earth he had chosen me I really do not know but the idea was to see how the body recovered from pain. They wanted to see me get bruised or cut and then watch how my body healed itself over time. Unfortunately for them, I had barely been caught in recent fights and didn't have a scratch on me. I think they were getting a bit frustrated and it was probably costing them a fortune to keep filming with me, but they had met me in Ireland on the Friday before the fight and we did a couple more interviews. I didn't love a camera crew following me around but at least it was a distraction from drinking. That was until they fucked off about 5pm and said they would see me at the fight the next day. That was my cue to get on the booze.

I managed to hide my hangover when Frank arrived the next day but the fight didn't go to plan. Me and Prunty clashed heads and the fight had to be stopped. I didn't box for a month after that, the usual 28-day ban applying and, with the cut needing to heal, it meant I couldn't spar either.

On my return I fought a lad called Stephen Ormond and Frank was on his own in the corner for the first time. That came with a lot of responsibility, because if your fighter was cut or injured then you had to deal with that. Likewise, if you felt your man had taken enough punishment, you had to decide whether to call off the fight and pull him out. The safety and wellbeing of the fighter is in your hands, at least in terms of some of the big decisions and reactions, if not the actual fight itself.

Frank was excited to be in the corner and set out his usual game plan: circle to the right to keep out of the way of his right hand, be nice and busy, hands high to protect the face. He was looking the part as well, was Frank. Carl had made up some t-shirts with my name on the back. They were white with red lettering and Frank was wearing his as he ushered me into the ring, an air of confidence about him with a bucket for my spit and bottle of water under his arm. He was guiding me through the crowd and talking to me the whole time:

'Just ignore all these cunts, bruv. Focus on what you need to do.'

I had a smart new pair of silky boxing shorts in the West Ham colours of claret and sky blue. On the belt line it read VICKI in sequins. I was punching myself in the face to keep myself alert, my usual pre-fight ritual.

My opponent called himself 'the Rock' and, although that was a bit premature considering he had only had six fights, he would go on to box for a European title, so he had a bit about him.

The first round went according to plan though and I was keeping out of the way of any big shots, following Frank's instructions. But right on the bell he swung a big right hand which skimmed and grazed the side of my head. It wobbled me a little but the round ended and I headed back to the corner to gather myself. Boxers get one minute between rounds which isn't long but that time can be precious when you've been hurt.

I sat down and Frank got out the towel to wipe the sweat off my head. As he smeared it over me, I felt a sharper pain and blood ran down my cheek. I'd been cut. Frank was panicking. He hadn't seen the cut when I'd sat down and had run the dry towel right over the wound, opening it up even worse.

'How bad is it?' I asked.

Now, any cornerman worth his salt would try to calm his fighter down and reassure them. But Frank was new to the game and all over the place.

'It's fucking awful,' he said. 'It's an inch long, John, and really deep.'

The blood kept flowing out of the wound and into my eyes. Frank was frantically trying to dab it down with a towel but only succeeding in making it worse. He had brought his bottle of adrenaline and some swabs but they were in the bottom of the bag. Adrenaline is what you apply to a cut to stop the blood flow but Frank hadn't prepared properly and couldn't find it in his bag. I was getting more annoyed now.

'For fuck's sake Frank, do something.'

He was running out of time so smeared some Vaseline on the wound and sent me back out for the second round. I would have to try to get through it until Frank had sorted himself out. I was swinging out of the way of punches and trying to focus on the fight but out of the corner of my eye I could see Frank, pulling everything out of the bag, desperately trying to find the adrenaline bottle.

It was a bad cut and it didn't take much to open it up even more. Ormond could see how bad it was and was doing all he could to target that area. At the end of the round I was covered in blood and this time Frank got to work, stemming the flow by pressing hard on the wound with the adrenaline-soaked swab.

'Sort yourself out, soppy bollocks!' I shouted.

'Fuck you!' he shouted back, clearly embarrassed.

The adrenaline did the trick and I managed to get to the end of the fight without the cut getting any worse but that was a huge learning curve for Frank. He needed to be ready at all times, because I was always in danger. Worse still, I was a bleeder. My skin seemed to open up easily and once I did get cut, there was always a lot of blood. Frank told me this was due to me being dehydrated and said I needed to drink more water before fights. I'm not sure if that was true or he was just trying to deflect attention away from his fuck-up.

Either way, Team Greaves was off to a bad start and it didn't get much better against Maxi Hughes. Maxi was an excellent fighter who fought for the British title a couple of times and was a really good, solid lad. This was his debut and on the way up to Doncaster, where the fight was being held, Frank devised a game plan to rough him up and give him a hard introduction to the professional fight game.

'Let's have a real go from the first bell and put it on him,' he said. 'He probably ain't that good and he won't have fought anyone like you before.'

This was how I spent most Friday or Saturday afternoons – sat in the back of Frank's black cab and listening to him talk tactics over the intercom as we travelled up the M1, usually stopping for a slash and a coffee on the way. I would keep Frank waiting while I had a fag and he would look at me out of the window, shaking his head disapprovingly or going into a rant about not looking after myself.

Doncaster was a good four-hour drive from London and the journey went slowly but as we got closer I began to get that feeling of anxiety in my stomach. Doncaster wasn't a place I was familiar with but the venue was quite cool. The Doncaster Dome was a modern building with palm trees outside and looked more like something you might find on the Las Vegas strip and not in deepest Yorkshire. There was a swimming pool and ice rink but that had been covered over and turned into a boxing arena for the night. It was a bigger show than I had imagined and Hughes had sold a lot of tickets judging by the crowd.

As we faced off in the ring and the referee gave us our instructions, there were cries all around the ring of 'Yorkshire, Yorkshire'. Maxi was a local lad and they wanted to see him start his professional career with a statement win. 'Fuck him up, get into him,' came the shouts from ringside as the fight began.

Frank was still a novice trainer so was taking a lot of the stick from the crowd personally, and was shouting back and trying to stand up for me. He went through the game plan one last time:

'Rough him up and show him what professional boxing is all about.'

I started as we had agreed, throwing quick shots and combinations, getting right in his face. Quick as a flash, he stepped back, changed the angle and caught me with a razor-sharp three-punch combination. I looked over and saw Frank's face change.

I got back to the corner at the end of the first round.

'Yeh, fuck that,' said Frank. 'We need to change tactics and get out of the fucking way of these punches, he's too good.'

Frank's masterplan had lasted a full two minutes. I managed to adapt and keep him at arm's length for most of the fight but Frank was getting a crash course in professional boxing. As well as getting his tactics completely wrong he was now engaged in a heated argument with some of Maxi's fans, offering them outside for a fight.

There was no way I was getting to 100 fights if this carried on. Something had to change and, as luck would have it, the boxing gods were listening to us.

Chapter Eleven

It's the Hope That Kills You

25 September 2010

Fight 57

Johnny Greaves v Floyd Moore
Fleming Park Leisure Centre, Eastleigh

Little Teddy had been given such a tough start in life but he was a fighter like me. He'd been through so many operations and even had his legs in braces for a time, which he really struggled with, but he was walking on his own now, albeit with a slight limp. He could easily have been self-conscious or felt different to other kids but he never showed it and was determined to do the same things that everyone else did. There was a real determination and strength about him. I felt so proud. I always wanted him to feel that way about me but all he had ever seen was Daddy coming back from fights with cuts and bruises. He would ask me if I'd won and by now I thought it was better to be honest, even if he seemed a bit disappointed when I told him the result.

He had just started primary school when I got offered a fight down near Southampton against a bloke called Floyd Moore. The money on offer was better than the going rate as this was what was known as a 'carry job' or 'walk around'. A carry job is when you have a young fighter making his professional debut and the promoter wants it to be an easy night's work. In other words, make him look good. Apparently, he had sold around 300 tickets, which was half the crowd, so the golden goose was most certainly not for killing. Not that it was bent or anyone told me to take it easy as such, but it was made clear that this lad could really do with a win. I knew what they meant by now.

My journey to every leisure centre in the UK was almost complete and now I could tick Fleming Park, Eastleigh, off the list as well. The venue and atmosphere reminded me of some of my early fights. There were no future world champions on this card, just a few local lads who had drummed up a bit of support. Most of the crowd seemed to be there for my opponent and, with it being his debut, there appeared to be a lot of excitement about what he might be capable of. He got the big build-up from the ring announcer and came charging out of his dressing room, well-built with a dark beard and hunched shoulders, pushing his way through the crowded ring apron and bowing to his adoring supporters. He looked really focused and fired up but I had seen so many fighters look like that so I just stood taking it all in without much emotion.

I could tell he was nervous because he was jumping around and throwing loads of air punches, talking to the fans around him, looking for reassurance from the team in his corner. This was classic debut behaviour and he needed to calm down or he would burn himself out. He was using up a lot of energy, bouncing about and whipping up the crowd.

He looked pretty lean and well prepared but boxing requires a certain kind of fitness and when you're very nervous you can 'gas' as they say in boxing. That means you use up too much nervous energy and run out of steam earlier than you would normally. It can look to the crowd like you haven't trained or are chronically unfit but that's often not the case.

Floyd was champing at the bit as the referee brought us together and as soon as the fight started he was throwing big haymakers and trying to knock my head off.

'Easy mate,' I said under my breath and looked at the promoter, as if to ask what was going on.

Clearly nobody had told Floyd that this was a move around and he was going full out for a stoppage. I avoided the shots that I could, held him a bit, threw the odd combination back to look busy, but I could see he was blowing already. He must have thrown close to 200 punches in the first round and could barely walk back to his corner. There was no way he was going to get through four rounds. No chance. I looked at the promoter again and shrugged my shoulders as if to say 'what can I do?' He looked concerned.

Second round and Floyd was still swinging and missing but by now the venom had gone out of his punches and he was puffing hard, desperately sucking in air. He was covered in sweat and it was pouring off his beard on to the canvas. I got in close for a clinch and decided to try and communicate with him, away from the earshot of the referee.

'For fuck's sake, ease up, Floyd,' I said.

He was completely immersed in his own world and still intent on knocking me out but there was no power in his punches at all. He had used up all his reserves of energy already. I was literally propping him up. The bell went and the referee came over to our corner to speak to me and Frank.

'I can see what you're doing in there. Throw some punches or I'll kick you out,' he said, and walked off as if meaning business.

Frank looked at me. 'Just hold him up, let him hit you, and make sure he fucking wins.'

By the fourth round he was like a fag paper in the wind. If I had blown on him hard enough he would have gone over. The crowd had quietened down and his supporters were looking concerned. I had my hands up high and was willing him to throw a punch to my body.

'Floyd mate, you HAVE to do something,' I shouted at him again.

But he was exhausted and couldn't hear a thing. As he rested his head on my shoulder, I pretended to throw some body shots but the referee wasn't stupid and pulled us apart again, urging us to fight properly.

The final bell sounded and I looked over at the promoter again. He was sweating and looked really anxious. This kid was the money-maker. He had to win or there wouldn't be another show with his name on anytime soon. You couldn't lose on your debut and still convince people that you were a future star that was worth supporting.

The referee started to walk over to me and I tried not to catch his eye. I almost ran away but he caught me and raised my hand. The ring announcer said the words that nobody in the venue wanted to hear, including me:

'Your winner, from East Ham, Johnny Greaves.'

One or two people clapped, the rest just hung their heads or filed out of the arena disappointed. Floyd could barely walk unaided out of the ring, looking on the verge of collapse, and seemed oblivious to what had happened.

These were the moments I had craved when I started boxing and yet I felt devastated. The promoter was fuming, more with Floyd than me I think, but I didn't work for him again for a long, long time. Perhaps it wasn't my fault but I hadn't done the job he was paying me for and I'd have to suffer the consequences.

The next morning I had a bit of a lie-in as we hadn't got home until the early hours. I could hear Teddy and Ruby playing and smiled at the thought of telling them Daddy had won a fight. I went downstairs and sat with them in the sitting room. Ruby was on my lap and started climbing all over me, poking my bruised eyes. 'Does that hurt?' she was saying as she tested the different areas. She was still a toddler, with curly blonde hair and such a sweet little face. I don't suppose seeing her dad in that state made much sense to her but she was becoming used to it and I would always say I was alright and not in pain, whether that was true or not.

Then Teddy told me he had something for me. He ran upstairs and returned with something he had made at school. When he came back down, I told him that I had won last night and boxed well. He had a big grin on his face and passed me the piece of paper he had been holding. On the front there was a picture of me that he had printed off the internet with 'My Sporting Hero' written along the top in big letters. He told me they had been asked to do a project at school about their sporting hero. Teddy had chosen me.

I gave him the biggest hug and tears came to my eyes. I felt something unusual. It took me a while to work it out but then it came to me. It was pride. In Teddy as my son and pride in myself. It was a feeling I didn't recognise.

13 November 2010

Fight 60

Johan Perez v Johnny Greaves
MEN Arena, Manchester

The win against Floyd Moore and making Teddy proud was a big lift emotionally, and on top of that, I was enjoying having Frank around as well.

We had been so different as kids. He was always quite a wise owl and saw his future as being away from East Ham. He was intelligent and sharp, doing well in his exams and making a stable life for himself as a cabbie and boxing trainer, as well as doing some work in TV. He was ambitious and knew how to push himself. He was all the things I wanted to be but never could.

Frank was also more emotionally secure than me. He knew how to look after himself and make good decisions. He would prefer to talk his way out of an argument when we were growing up whereas I would go steaming into a fight without thinking.

There was one occasion when Frank got glassed in the face in a nightclub. We were probably in our late teens at the time and got into an argument with a group of lads at the bar. One of their lot decided to be the peacemaker and suggested to Frank that they shake hands and move on. Frank being a bit more reasonable than me, held his hand out, and the fella stuck a broken glass into the side of his face. There was blood everywhere and me and the rest of my mates tore into them as Frank lay there in shock.

That situation would never have happened to me. If that bloke had held his hand out to me, I would have smacked him in the mouth. Not because I wanted to be a tough guy but because life taught me to fight first and ask questions later.

I could never walk away from conflict if I had even the slightest sense I was being disrespected.

There was another time in my 20s when a bloke in a pub got a bit aggressive and called me a cunt. I felt the rage rising up in my chest but for once I decided to be the better man and go home. I felt really proud of myself for walking away. This was the new, mature Johnny. But as I got changed and slipped into bed, I could feel it eating away at me. Who was he to call me a cunt? I tried to sleep but couldn't. After 20 minutes it got the better of me. I jumped out of bed, got changed, walked back into town, found the bloke in the pub and gave him a proper hiding. The feeling in my body of being wronged was too overpowering. It almost made me feel physically sick and I would have to do something about it to make that feeling go away. That's why I needed some guidance and some balance in my life. I think Frank and I both hoped that he would provide that.

Frank 'the Professor' Greaves, I started calling him. He would always be in a tracksuit, blonde hair swept back with a mountain of wax, shades on. He was a handsome bastard and still is. I was always jealous of that too. Good-looking lad, bright, articulate, charming. I must have been at the bottom of the pile when they were handing out the family genes.

As he was driving me up the motorway in his cab to a fight, he would say things like, 'Johnny, tonight just stay on the back foot, keep your distance, left hand nice and high, don't take any chances.'

His advice always went against my instincts, which were to stand and have a fight. I'd be sat there in a daydream, feeling depressed or suicidal, smoking fags out of the window, much to his annoyance. He would tell me I was fighting a solid kid who could punch.

'Don't stand and fight the kid, you aren't getting paid any more to get hit, what's the point? Use your brain. Get in there and box.'

Often, at the end of a first round when I had completely disregarded the game plan we had agreed, Frank would scream at me:

'For FUCK'S SAKE, what the fuck are you doing?'

He would be exasperated and wondering why I was employing the opposite tactics to the ones we had spoken about. I tried to listen but I boxed on emotions. Frank had worked with fighters for years but hadn't been in a professional ring before. He would see it as a chess match rather than a gladiatorial battle and so we would argue all the time.

I was downbeat and depressive most of the time, struggling to see the good in life. He was naturally positive by nature and couldn't understand my outlook.

'Cheer the fuck up,' he would say constantly. 'What the fuck have you got to feel miserable about?' But I don't think he really understood how dark it was in my head.

The fight against Johan Perez was one bout where I needed all of Frank's guidance and support, for one good reason: Perez was the most fearsome puncher I had ever faced. Now bear in mind I'd had baseball bats and car jacks wrapped around my skull, but nothing compared to this bloke. He was a beast, a freak. This was a knockout merchant extraordinaire. He was putting people to sleep in almost every fight and would eventually go on to become world champion, beating Fernando Castaneda to win the WBA light welterweight title. He would have a second reign as world champion as well when beating the previously unbeaten Paul Spadafora, so that tells you what a classy operator he was.

At this point he was only ten fights into his professional career with seven knockouts but word had got around the circuit that he was vicious. The Venezuelan went by the name of 'El Terrible', which didn't bode well for me.

After seeing the size of him at the weigh-in and with his knockout record, I felt like a lamb to the slaughter. He was tall and rangy with long arms covered in tattoos and sharp features that made him look like a Bond villain.

The WBA had organised the fight to give Perez some overseas experience. He looked twice the size of me and when he stood on the scales I understood why. He was three pounds over, which might not sound like a lot but by the time of the fight the next day, once he had rehydrated and eaten well, he would likely be a stone heavier than me and that would be way too much of an advantage. His power already gave him enough of one. I couldn't be giving away that kind of weight as well.

I would probably have just cracked on and accepted the fight but Frank wasn't having it.

'He needs to take that weight off or we go home,' Frank told Perez's team.

They didn't look happy and even offered us a bit more money to fight. I would have bitten their hand off but Frank stuck to his guns.

'Nah thanks. Weight off or we leave.'

There was always pressure on journeymen to box, whatever the circumstances. The promoters and home fighters would try these kinds of tricks, believing that we needed the money and would fight under any conditions. Perez and his team were not impressed but Frank was insistent, looking out for my safety and knowing they couldn't get a replacement at this stage.

So in the end we stood there watching while Perez ran up and down in the hotel lobby, doing laps in his sweat-suit to shift the weight. You could tell he was embarrassed and his team were fuming but Frank had made his decision and wasn't leaving until Perez had lost those three pounds on the scales. Eventually, he tried again, stripping down so he was completely naked, and was just on the limit. We had succeeded in making sure it was a fair fight in terms of weight but now you could tell he was even more fired up. We had awoken the beast.

The fight was on the undercard of the big David Haye versus Audley Harrison bout – two heavyweights who were generating a lot of noise in the UK at the time. George Groves was also fighting and the event was live on Sky so Manchester was buzzing. We were staying at the very posh Lowry Hotel right in the centre of the city. That was where all the footballers stayed and it was covered in fine art, with a swanky restaurant full of celebrities who were in town for the boxing. It must have been booked by the promoter because there was no way I'd have paid for a place like that. My cousin Jason had tagged along to help out in the corner and the three of us didn't fit in at all, decked out in tracksuits and scruffy jeans, so we decided to go round the corner to TGI Fridays for some food. It had been quite a stressful afternoon all things considered and I really fancied a pint to calm myself down. Frank wasn't happy, though.

'You're not having a pint, John. Did you not see the size of the geezer earlier? You need to be as sharp as possible tomorrow,' he said sternly.

'Fucking hell Frank, relax mate, it's one pint,' I argued.

But Frank was having none of it. He was going all big brother on me, getting more and more irate, telling me that if I had a pint then I was on my own the next day. I didn't see what the big deal was. I always had a few drinks before a fight as it helped to calm me down. Frank hadn't been with me for most of my career so had no clue what I'd got up to. As far as he was concerned though, he was in charge of my corner and decided what I was putting in my body.

I had the arsehole with him and we barely spoke during dinner. Once we got back to the hotel, Frank and Jason went to the bar.

'How comes you two can have a beer then?' I argued.

'Cos we ain't fighting, silly bollocks. Now get some rest. Tomorrow is a big day,' said Frank.

Fighting back against Gavin Tait

Covering up against Liam Walsh

Stopped by Liam Walsh

Taking punishment against Bradley Skeete

On the back foot against Bradley Skeete

Stopped by Skeete

Versus Jason Hastie

Taking a left hook against Stephen Ormond

Exchanging blows with Justin Newell

Sent sprawling by Peter McDonagh

A right hand from Justin Newell through the guard

Johnny battles bravely against Bradley Skeete

Skeete landing a long right hand

On the canvas after being knocked down by Skeete

Inconsolable after loss to Bradley Skeete

Fighting back tears after final fight

HOME   POLITICS   COMMUNITY   SPORTS   ENTERTAINMENT   CULTURE   CRI

⌂ Home / Sports / Johnny Greaves awarded manager's licence

Johnny Greaves awarded manager's licence

🕓 November 23, 2015   💬 5

After 100 professional boxing fights, earning the title of "King of the Journeyman", East-Ender Johnn Greaves has begun the next chapter of his boxing story. The 36-year-old, who bowed out from the ranks with a win over Dan Carr in September 2013, has recently received his manager's licence from British Boxing Board of Control (BBBofC).

Greaves has been spending his time out of the ring training the next generation of professional box his home away from home – the Peacock Gym in Canning Town. "It's the second page of my profes boxing journey," said Greaves. "The first steps are for me to get established, attract new boxers, an start putting on my own shows. I've been in the Peacock Gym since I was 10-years-old and I've rub shoulders with a lot of people and managers like Dean Powell.

"I just want to get the best out of my boys. Fighters don't get paid enough and it's good for them t someone like me in their corner, fighting for them. It'll be nice to make a living from boxing but it w out of love rather than for money and it'll be for the good of the fighters."

Follow Johnny on Twitter at @johnnygreaves

Johnny would like to thank his sponsors and PR Manager Tim Rickson.

I sloped off upstairs to my room, berating myself for ever getting Frank involved. It was more fun on my own. I could do what the fuck I wanted then. The more I thought about it, the more annoyed I got. Who the fuck was Frank to tell me what I could and couldn't do? I'd managed 59 fights without him and survived this long.

I called down to room service and ordered a couple of Peronis. If I was going to get carried out of that ring on a stretcher, then I might as well enjoy tonight. I remember sticking on an old re-run of *Only Fools and Horses* and at some point ordering another couple of beers. After that everything went blank.

I don't remember getting to breakfast the next day but I do recall feeling nervous and had a bit of anxiety as the effects of the alcohol wore off. We were due to leave at 3pm so had plenty of time to kill. I needed to get some more rest so went back upstairs for a lie down. The place was a state. I couldn't remember drinking that much. I crashed on the bed and came round to the sound of Frank knocking on the door.

'Let me in,' he said. 'We need to leave in ten minutes. I'll help carry your bags down.'

Fuck. I looked around and the room was covered in empty bottles, glasses and fag butts. Frank was knocking hard now and trying to get me to open up. He could tell something was wrong.

'Give me a minute bruv, for fuck's sake. I've only just woken up,' I said.

'Fine, meet me in the lobby soon as possible then,' Frank replied, suspiciously.

We got to the venue and I was even more emotional than usual. I'd drunk to avoid thinking and feeling but now both were back with interest. My head was working overtime: was I about to be brutally knocked out? What would Frank do if he found out about last night? Would the board take away my licence?

The MEN Arena was filling up. It was a brilliant venue that always seemed to sell out for the big fights. Ricky Hatton had been a regular there during his career and his fans had always turned it into a wall of noise. Mike Tyson had also fought Julius Francis here in a fight that had got a lot of publicity, not least because he threatened to throw Frank Warren out of a hotel window in the build-up. It reminded me a bit of the O2 Arena: really steep seating either side of the ring but everyone feeling like they were almost on top of you. Twenty thousand people would be there to watch the action unfold but we had no idea when we would be fighting.

Our bout was what's known as a 'floater' which means a fight that can be scheduled at any time, right until the last minute. On the big shows they are always working to the timings of the broadcasters and, because you don't know in advance how long each contest will take, sometimes you need to squeeze in another fight so that the main event is broadcast at peak time. That means you have to be ready to fight from really early on in the evening but might not actually be called out until last. It's very hard to prepare and keep your focus.

I was praying we would be on nice and late. That would give me time to fully sober up and get myself together. I got my wish but the downside was that we were told we would be on just before the big fight of the evening, which meant the arena would be packed. There was nowhere to hide for me now. David Haye and Audley Harrison were getting ready to come out and entertain the crowd and I was going to be the hors d'oeuvre.

I walked out and the place was absolutely jumping. There wasn't an empty seat anywhere. They'd all come to watch the two big heavyweights, so when my name was called out there was an audible groan from the crowd. They didn't want to have to sit through another contest between two blokes they had never heard of. The promoters and the TV people must all have been hoping I would get sparked out early. A quick one- or two-rounder with a dramatic finish would be the ideal warm-up for the main fight.

Perez had clearly read the script because in the first round he came charging at me. I went to sidestep the shot and roll underneath but my body didn't seem to be responding as well as normal. I couldn't get out of the way and he landed cleanly with the first shot he threw. It thudded into the side of my head and the pain was crippling. There was also an ominous thudding sound as it connected with my temple.

I could hear Jason and Frank go 'ooooh' and looked around to see them wincing.

163

'Fuck off you pair of cunts, turn it in!' I screamed.

This was bad enough already without those two adding commentary and sound effects.

When you get caught around the temple it's disorientating and those are the punches that put you down. The ones you see coming can hurt or sting but you can sometimes ride those out but this guy was different. I knew that if he caught me clean, it was lights out.

The crowd were loving it and dying to see me on the canvas so the main fight wouldn't be delayed any longer. I dug deep and pulled out every trick in the book to try to fend him off – holding, using my head, punching him in the bollocks. At one point I even kicked him in the shin. I looked at him and laughed but he wasn't seeing the funny side. He kept coming forward, throwing endless combinations and doing all he could to take me out.

Every punch was hurting but the adrenaline kept me going. The fight had been reduced from six rounds to four at the last minute as the broadcasters didn't want to delay the main event, and that is what saved me. The extra two rounds would have finished me off but four I could just about handle. I knew there wasn't long left and just grabbed hold of him as hard as I could. The referee was trying to separate us and get us to box on but I was done.

At the final bell Perez came walking over with a confused look on his face. I thought he was going to knock me out as retribution for all my antics during the fight but instead he gave me a big hug and pointed at his head: 'Loco,' he said, meaning crazy. I smiled back and gave him a wink.

I was already feeling the effects when we got back to the hotel after the fight. My ribs were sore and my head was banging. Frank offered to carry my bags back to the room and I was grateful for the help. I could barely stand up straight and like an idiot, I'd forgotten what a state the room was in. I opened the door and it was like a scene from *Armageddon*. Frank was fucking fuming. There must have been a good six empty pint glasses and a bottle of red on the side.

'You stupid fucking bastard,' said Frank, and walked out in disgust.

10 December 2010

Fight 63
Tony Owen v Johnny Greaves
Savoy Hotel, London

I was now at my lowest ebb since I had started boxing professionally around three and a half years earlier. I had completed 60 fights, losing 57 of them, and the physical and emotional scars were becoming harder to mask. The fights were getting much more difficult, the damage to my body and my psyche taking longer and longer to repair after each defeat, and on top of that I was putting myself in more and more danger with each passing fight. I was a ticking time-bomb.

The Perez loss drained me in so many ways, not least financially. They paid me with a post-dated cheque that I couldn't cash until a few weeks later so, with Christmas not far away, I had to borrow some money from the old man. He was ok about it but it made me feel even more like a failure. I was 30 years old and fighting on big TV shows, yet still having to go and scrounge from my dad.

That feeling of worthlessness returned. It never left me for long. So as the festive period approached, I started drinking more and training even less than usual. I wasn't eating properly either, so my weight dropped and I lost quite a lot of muscle mass. I looked pale and had bags under my eyes but I wasn't aware of just how much my appearance had changed until I saw Frank's reaction when we met up at the Savoy Hotel in London for a fight against Tony Owen.

He was on me straight away.

'What the fuck has happened to you? Look at the state of you!' Frank said.

I shrugged and said I was fine but he had seen me like this before and knew what it meant – booze and coke. We did the weigh-in at around 2pm and I was a few pounds lighter than normal. Frank took me aside for what I knew was going to be a big lecture. The Savoy was a posh place tucked away on the Strand with a fancy silver and gold entrance, marble floors and mahogany walls. People were pulling up in Bentleys and chucking their keys to the concierge, strutting around like peacocks. Frank and me didn't fit in here but it was peak tourist season outside and the streets were rammed so we found a little quiet area of the bar and tried to make ourselves inconspicuous.

He was telling me to get a hold of myself, to stop being selfish and think about the kids. How he wasn't prepared to stand by and watch me get hurt. That he would tell the board and they would revoke my licence. He was seriously concerned and I had to persuade him to even let me go ahead with the fight that evening.

I knew what he was saying was right but I felt the need to try and justify the way I looked. I told him that I'd been doing some labouring with Vicki's dad and we didn't get on so it had been stressful; how I was doing a lot of physical outdoor work, so that was probably why I'd dropped some weight. These stories were half true. The work was hard and could be stressful but I wasn't looking after myself either.

Frank looked like he was questioning himself. He'd become part of the team with the hope of getting me to fight sensibly and train harder, help me get to the 100 and retire with my faculties intact. This was not what he had signed up for.

'I'm alright, don't worry about me,' I said.

But I always said that. The truth was that I wasn't alright at all. Mentally I was much more brittle that I had been previously and my body felt weak too. I was struggling with sore ribs, a hangover from the Perez fight, and told Frank I would have to cover up and try to protect them. One solid shot to that area and I would be out for months.

Ribs were the worst part of the body to get hit. You could barely move if you cracked a rib – even going to the toilet was agony. So we changed my style a bit for the fight and worked on some ideas to protect that area. This was now becoming a regular part of the fight preparation – managing my body and the various cuts and bruises. I was getting hurt more often and stopped more regularly but even with the 28-day bans, I didn't have enough time to heal. I was staggering from one fight to the next and picking up more injuries along the way.

Tony Owen was a big lad too with a strong frame, ginger-haired and rugged-looking. He had been a very decent amateur and was fresh and sharp, throwing a lot of punches. We were one of only three fights on the bill so the crowd, all sat at round tables and being served a three-course meal while the boxing took place, wanted to get their money's worth. It wasn't a pressure fight like the one against Perez. There were no TV cameras and only a couple of hundred people, plus Owen was a level down as an opponent, but I was finding it just as tough. I was covering up the ribs and being very conservative with my work, struggling through and racking up another loss. Johnny Greaves, beaten on points. They would be writing that on my headstone one day.

Maybe I didn't know it at the time, but this was the beginning of the end for me as a professional boxer. My body and mind were no longer willing. Frank and I never spoke about it but there was now a silent agreement between us that the rest of the journey would be solely about survival and nothing more. I was finished but I couldn't let anyone else see that. Not the promoters nor my opponents, and certainly not Vicki. If she knew how I was really feeling she would have put a stop to it. The problem was, there was still a long way to go to get to the 100.

Chapter Twelve

Breaking Down

11 February 2011

Fight 64

Johnny Greaves v Bradley Skeete
York Hall, Bethnal Green

Boxing always takes a break after Christmas and, while I missed the extra money, that period allowed my body to heal a bit. I was still up and down, struggling with the dark days of January and February, when I would be awake before first light travelling to a painting job somewhere, then coming home in the dark later on. But I was a little better in myself physically for the rest. My ribs had healed and some of the cuts around my eyes, although heavily damaged and now mainly just scar tissue and prone to opening up again, weren't so prominent.

From a mental perspective I really needed a fight. Those bleak winter months were difficult times for me. My bones ached in the cold, I was getting arthritis in my hands and fingers from punching too much, which made my job a real challenge, and emotionally things felt really bleak. There was very little to look forward to. Life was just an endless grind. So the thought of getting back in the ring gave me a little bit of hope. A reason to get up the next day and keep going.

I could have done with a couple of nice easy ones to start the year but the first fight I had been offered was set to be a tough one, against a fighter called Bradley Skeete, who wasn't known for his knockout power but was very tall and slick with a big reach. I never did well against guys like that.

I remember the late Dean Powell, a matchmaker and trainer who worked for Frank Warren for many years, saying to me: 'Don't worry about the size, he can't crack an egg.'

That meant he couldn't punch, but I was always dubious about that because knockout power and being able to land hurtful shots are two very different things. Until you have shared a ring with someone, you really don't know.

Skeete was part of the Frank Warren stable and they had high hopes for him. They wanted to build his profile, starting with a nice easy fight against yours truly. We both weighed 10st 4lb but by the day of the fight, a bit like Perez, he must have been about a stone heavier. These are the quirks of boxing and weights. You can occasionally get fighters who are naturally big in terms of frame but don't weigh as much as other people their size. That's a huge advantage because on the day of the fight, once they have refuelled, they are even bigger and heavier. I probably only put on a few pounds between the weigh-in and the fight itself. I was a natural lightweight whereas he could have piled on a few pounds and fought at welterweight or even super welterweight quite comfortably.

Not only was he much bigger than me but stylistically, Skeete was going to be all wrong for me as well. He was skilful, quick, clever and fought at long range. I liked guys who wanted to mix it and go to war.

Brad was a lovely lad though, not intimidating or scary in any way. Quite an intelligent, thoughtful chap. I liked him. I think we even had a bit of banter in the build-up to the fight as it was due to be on TV and we had to do some media. I was acting the clown and loving the limelight. He looked a bit bemused, but there was no edge. He even thanked me for taking the fight.

He stood next to me before the first bell and looked massive. He was about 6ft 3in so towering over me and his knuckles were nearly touching the canvas. The first shot he hit me with was a jab and it got my attention immediately because it seemed to come from about a mile away. My brain couldn't compute it: how had he landed that punch from there? It caught me right on the end of the nose and, despite all the talk about him having no power, I felt it alright. My eyes started to water straight away and I knew it was going to be a long night.

My cousin Jason was helping Frank in the corner once again. Jason has always been a man who speaks his mind and doesn't hold back. He's a big, scary-looking fella with a shaved head and pock-marked face, but he was clearly worried about my safety after just one punch had been thrown.

'Try to stay out the way of his jab!' he shouted.

I stared at him.

'What do you think I'm trying to fucking do?!'

Skeete looked bemused. He would never have seen anything quite like this in the amateur game. I hoped it might distract him and knock him off his rhythm but no such luck. He was focused and intent on getting a stoppage to start his professional career. He was a big lad but moved really well, precise with his footwork and thoughtful about which shots to throw. He would circle around me, out of reach and working out his angles, then he would throw punches that seemed to find their target every time. His reach was like nothing I had faced before. Every time I thought I was out of range, he would catch me. Over and over. His arms were like tentacles and when the punch is travelling that distance, it carries some spite.

In the second round I got put down with a long straight shot. I just didn't see it coming and couldn't react in time. Before I knew it, I was on the canvas and being counted out by the referee. I managed to get up at about six or seven, holding on to the ropes to steady my legs. I wasn't badly hurt but when you don't see the punch coming it discombobulates you. Your brain can't work out what has happened and that's why you get knocked out sometimes.

I stood and looked at the referee, giving him a nod to say I was ok. I had a quick glance at Frank and Jason, who both looked concerned. I mouthed at them that I was fine and bobbed up and down on the spot to get my legs going. All I could hear was Frank and Jason telling me to use my feet, stay out of the way. I knew that was good advice but it's debilitating to keep taking so many punches and you start to slow down.

I did my best to keep him off me but in round three he floored me again with a left hook to the body. Fuck.

Frank said I looked visibly shaken. He had been with me at a lot of fights and rarely seen me in serious trouble but this was different. I tried to gather myself and get to my feet again but stumbled forward, struggling to find my balance, and the referee quickly waved off the contest. I had been stopped for only the second time in my career.

Afterwards, I was really tearful and kept apologising to anyone who would talk to me. To Frank and Jason, to Bradley and his team, to the fans in the bar. I always felt like I had let people down but as a boxer I became accustomed to getting through fights at the very least. Being stopped wasn't part of the act. I didn't get stopped. I was Johnny Greaves. Or at least I had been.

Bradley was very sweet about it and came over for a chat. He said what a hard night I had given him. I think he was being generous but I needed to hear those words. I was telling anyone who would listen that he was too big and should be fighting at a bigger weight. That was true, but it also gave me an excuse and stopped me focusing on my own issues. It stopped me confronting the truth – that

I was losing my toughness and resilience. When that's all you've ever had, it's a hard thing to accept.

The Olympic gold medallist James DeGale was a friend of Bradley's and had come to watch the fight. He came bowling over to see Bradley, laughing and smirking, completely oblivious to the fact that I was stood there and had just been beaten. He didn't do anything wrong at all but in a heartbeat I lost my shit. He was about three stone heavier than me and a world champion in the making but I didn't care. Who the fuck was he to laugh in my face?

'You think it's funny you cunt, I'll bite your fucking nose off.'

DeGale looked shocked and told me to calm down but I wasn't having that.

'Fuck off you cunt,' I spat, and was ushered away by security before I got involved with my second fight of the night.

I said nothing on the way home in Frank's cab. I was devastated. Frank was reassuring me that it was all due to the size difference and that I wouldn't have to fight guys like him every week. But the voices in my head were back.

'You're a fucking loser. I thought you were tough? You just got humiliated. You're shit. A shit boxer and a shit husband and dad. Now what are you going to do? You've got no money and no prospects. What's the point of carrying on?'

It was always the same narrative, on repeat. I was used to hearing it but having been stopped, somehow it felt even more real.

175

'Just end it. That would be best for everyone,' said the voice.

In the fights that followed there was one issue after another, and it was hard to tell what was mental and what was physical. I returned to the ring against Francis Robinson – the son of former world featherweight champion Steve Robinson – and while I negotiated the fight without too many dramas, I had an issue with my eye in the changing room afterwards. During the post-fight check-up, the doctor was worried that the eye wasn't responding to light and they wanted to send me to hospital for an MRI scan. He was concerned that I might have an underlying neurological issue, which scared the shit out of me. Was my brain fucked from taking too many punches? I knew it was, to be honest. I could feel my speech changing and memory going, but I couldn't stop fighting yet. Not before the 100. The 100 was more important than my health. In the end I convinced him to send me home and the eye seemed to clear up but I should have heeded the warning, taken some time off and let it heal properly. But fights just seemed to follow me wherever I went.

I had agreed to help out in the corner of another journeyman boxer by the name of Jody Meikle. He was a wild character, not too dissimilar to me: bald head but much heavier and game for fighting anyone you could put in front of him. He was another fighter on Carl's books and we had got to know each other when fighting on the same shows. Double-hard bastard was Jody and a guy I had a lot of time for.

I was getting Jody taped up and ready for his fight when the promoter, Micky Helliet, came over looking flustered.

'What are you weighing, John?' he asked.

I told him I was around my usual weight of 10st 7lb, which was bollocks as I hadn't been training and felt noticeably heavier. Micky told me that there had been a late pull-out and that he was desperate for an opponent. He said the kid was called Eren Arif and it was his debut. I wasn't really in the mood and was making my excuses but he told me the guy was nervous and it would be an easy night for me.

I saw the pound signs straight away and didn't need any more convincing. We did a very quick weigh-in and I was a full 10lb heavier than my opponent, which was a huge advantage. But Micky knew what I was like and that I would play the game rather than go full out for the win. By that point, I was barely capable anyway.

I didn't have any boxing kit with me so I rung Vicki. She was less than impressed but agreed to drive my kit to Chadwell Heath station and I would pick it up. The fight wasn't due on until later in the evening so I had just about enough time to go and get back. I grabbed the bag and headed to Bethnal Green on the tube but when I arrived at York Hall and started to get myself ready, I realised there was no gumshield. If you don't know boxing then a gumshield is a crucial bit of kit for protecting your teeth. Every fighter has their own which is moulded to their teeth to ensure maximum protection. Fuck. Time was getting tight now so I looked around and found my mate and trainer Ian Burbage, who had one of his fighters on the show. He found an old gumshield in his bag. I gave it a wash down and stuck it in my gob. It was completely the wrong size but I had no time left.

I knew it wasn't going to work but it was too late. I bit down on the gumshield and decided to keep away from as many punches as I could. He wasn't going to be anywhere near the level of Skeete so I wouldn't be taking as many shots, but you can't have a four-round fight and not get hit. As it was, the first punch he threw knocked both my front teeth out and wedged them into the gumshield. I could feel them snap away but had no choice other than to fight on, the adrenaline keeping the pain at bay.

I had made myself some unexpected money but now all that cash would be going on getting two new teeth fitted. The dentist told me that once you lose one tooth there is no bridge. That means that each time you take a punch, there is no stability and nothing to protect the teeth from snapping away again. So from that point on I just lost front tooth after front tooth, almost every fight, and ended up looking like a raving smackhead.

People laugh at that story when I tell them but it actually highlighted the lack of self-care I had. Nobody would be stupid enough to take a fight when they were so unprepared, never mind get in the ring without their gumshield. I didn't know how to say no. I didn't know how to look after myself. Or maybe I liked the danger, the thought of getting hurt and feeling that pain. Was this really about proving my toughness or some kind of death wish? Was my brain so damaged now that I couldn't think straight? Was it the booze and the coke? Or was I just a fuck-up, addicted to danger? I didn't even know the answer because I didn't know myself. I was just on a train heading for the end of the line and I couldn't stop it. Maybe I didn't want to.

Not long after that I took a fight against Liam Taylor, a boxer who would go on to fight for a British title. The event was up in Manchester and Frank had borrowed a car off his mate as a few of us were travelling up together. There was a bit of banter flying around and for a while it reminded me why I had started boxing in the first place. Then the turbo blew out and the car couldn't go faster than 30 miles per hour. We also missed our turning and so the journey ended up taking three hours longer than it should have done. My mood had darkened quite a bit by the time we arrived and the promoter told me that I would be fighting last. I was fuming and not in the headspace to be fucked around anymore. I was sick of boxing and the bullshit that went with it: nobody giving a fuck about me or what I wanted, just expecting me to play the game and be treated like a cunt. I wasn't sitting around until 10.30 at night and then having a six-hour journey home in a beaten-up motor.

'Fuck that, put me on early or I'm going home,' I said.

I started to pack my bags. The promoter could tell I was serious and knew that me walking out put the whole show in jeopardy.

'Alright, let me see what I can do,' he replied.

He came back 20 minutes later and said we could go on first.

Still, my head wasn't right. At that point I just wanted the fight over with and to get back on the road as soon as possible. I was taking the piss, not concentrating and getting caught by shot after shot. I was beating my chest and screaming at Taylor to bring it on. At the end of the first round, Frank was furious.

'What the fuck are you doing?' he shouted at me. 'John, he's got a lovely left hand, for fuck's sake stop walking on to it and get your hands up.'

I glared at him.

'I'll fucking do what I want, just give me a drink and shut the fuck up.'

Frank stared at me.

'Fuck you then, do what you want from now on, you cunt.'

He gave me a drink and didn't utter another word. I came back to the corner after the next round and there was silence.

'Well …?' I asked, looking for some guidance and advice.

'Well fucking what? You're on your own, bruv,' Frank sneered.

Nothing was said on the way home. Frank was seriously pissed off and I wasn't about to say sorry. We got hungry and stopped at a McDonalds on the M6. We were waiting for our food and Frank pulled me aside. I knew what was coming.

'If you want to keep standing in the way of shots and putting yourself in danger, then that's up to you bruv, but you're on your own. I'm not doing it anymore. I'm out.'

I could feel tears in my eyes. I knew what he was saying was right and I didn't want to lose Frank. I gave him a hug and said that I was sorry. I told him I was struggling mentally and promised to change. I meant it but deep down I knew I wasn't capable. That the emptiness I felt within would have to be filled by something.

I was mentally unwell and shouldn't have been fighting but nobody apart from Frank knew the extent of the problem and the promoters didn't care. Johnny Greaves was still a good booking. Maybe an even better one now he might get stopped or knocked out.

11 December 2011

Fight 77

Shayne Singleton v Johnny Greaves
Municipal Hall, Colne

My head was all over the place when I fought a guy called Shayne Singleton up in Lancashire. He was a good British-title level fighter but the type I had handled with ease in the early part of my career. However, now I was on the edge, fighting the demons in my mind and trying to find ways to cope. I was constantly emotional and reactive. One minute angry, then upset and sad, the next quiet and reflective. I wasn't mentally strong enough to cope with a packed-out arena all booing and jeering. I used to love it but now it just made me more anxious.

Singleton was naturally much bigger, and well-muscled, something that was becoming a theme. He had won all of his ten professional fights and was on the way up. My pal and sparring partner Dan Naylor was on the bill before me that night. We had travelled up together and he was on the end of a terrible decision, losing a fight on points that he clearly won. I had watched from ringside and that only made my mental state even worse. The injustice of boxing was starting to break me.

When it came to my turn to fight, it was clear early on that I didn't have the tools to keep Singleton off me, even for four rounds. The next time we got into a clinch, I punched him hard in the bollocks. He was winded and bent double, taking a step back and appealing to the referee to take action. He duly stepped in and had a stern word, threatening to take a point off me if I did anything like that again. He could take all the points off me for all I cared. I wasn't going to win in any case. As we broke to restart the fight, Singleton caught me flush on the chin with a cheeky punch. You don't do that in boxing and he knew it. He was just getting angry and seeking retribution for what I'd done. I was fuming and without thinking, I kicked him flush in the leg. The crowd were going mad and the referee looked utterly bemused. He stared at me and then over at Frank, shaking his head. He should have taken a point off me or even thrown me out but I don't think he had ever seen anything like it before.

He also knew my reputation for being overly emotional and was one of those who understood that us journeymen had it tough and needed the money. So somehow I was allowed to continue and see out the fight but that should have been a red flag to the board, Frank and me. I was in no state to be in a professional boxing ring.

There was the odd occasion when I put in a half-decent performance, like against Mark Ginley on a show in Belfast, but then I didn't get the decision and that just fuelled the resentment even more.

After that fight I got so fucked on booze and coke that Frank couldn't find me in the morning and we nearly missed our flight home. I hadn't even been to bed and didn't know where I was. He found me wandering around the hotel corridors and was going mad, telling me what a liability I was and how I needed to take a long look at myself. I could barely hear him and just shrugged and asked him if he had a cigarette, which tipped him over the edge.

'No I fucking haven't you cunt, now get in the car or I'll leave you here.'

I was in such a state that there was no way they would let me fly if they had taken a proper look at me. So Frank had to take my passport and I hid behind him like a little kid.

When I got home, the drink and drugs started wearing off and were replaced with that familiar feeling of anxiety. Vicki had gone up to bed and I was watching some shit on TV, trying to keep the negative feelings at bay but that sense of dread was just consuming me. I wandered upstairs, moving as quietly as I could so as not to disturb anyone. I opened the bathroom cabinet and found a big multi-pack of painkillers I usually used to cure hangovers. I took them downstairs and slowly took one by one, washing them down with lager each time. It was easy. Painless. I must have swallowed 15 or 20 tablets and could feel myself getting sleepy. It felt good, like a relief. I didn't know how many you needed to kill yourself, I just wanted to drift off. Like a nice sleep, I would close my eyes and wake up in a better place.

I was getting more and more drowsy, and then that was it. I was gone.

Or at least I thought I was until I opened my eyes and could hear the birds singing and the kids running around having breakfast and getting ready for school. I looked around bleary-eyed. I was definitely alive. And worse than that, I felt a million dollars. I must have taken just enough to send me off to sleep and take away any aches and pains as well. I was feeling a long way from dead. In fact, I wondered if 15 ibuprofen might be the answer every night. Hearing the kids, and away from the darkness and solitude of the night before, I was momentarily glad I was still alive but it wasn't long before the voices started up. 'What sort of dad leaves his kids? You can't love them. You can't love Vicki. Maybe you're just broken and not capable of love. Perhaps killing yourself would be the best thing. If you had the bollocks you would do it, you loser.' I hated myself before, but now the self-loathing was even worse.

Chapter Thirteen

Losing My Mind

10 March 2012

Fight 80

Terry Needham v Johnny Greaves

Olympia, Liverpool

I'd been booked to fight Terry Needham up in Liverpool and had three or four fights in the diary for the following weeks as well. If I could come through this little batch of fights unscathed then I would be making a good few quid and be getting closer to the 100. The way I was feeling physically and emotionally, retirement couldn't come quickly enough. Added to that was a strong sense that the board was starting to look at my fights more closely and with some concern.

The fight was at Olympia, a really smart arena with stalls and an upper circle making it feel like an old West End theatre. Then there was a big floor space where people could sit or stand, with the ring at the end like a cinema screen. Needham was a scouser so had a load of his supporters in the crowd. He was a thick-set, mean-looking bloke who reminded me of one of those nightclub bouncers I'd taken on in the past. He didn't have much of an amateur background and wasn't expected to go far in the professional game so it should have been a nice simple night's work.

I could tell early on he wasn't a banger so even in my fragile state, there was no way he was stopping me or knocking me out. But somehow in the first round we both tried to throw punches at the same time and our heads came together. I stepped back for a second, unsure of what damage we had inflicted, and touched the top of my head with my glove.

Blood. And a lot of it. I stared at him and could feel this rage rising up within me.

'You've fucking cut me, you cunt! You've just cost me four grand!'

He looked like he didn't have a clue what I was talking about but my head had gone. I would be getting a 28-day ban and all those fights would be cancelled.

I immediately set about him, shouting and swinging big shots. I was desperate to knock the cunt out. I wanted to get him back for what he had done to me. It became a bar brawl, fists and elbows flying and the referee in the middle trying to keep some kind of order.

The crowd were getting involved and calling me a cockney cunt. I was shouting back, poking my tongue out. Even Needham's mum was getting involved.

'Come on Terry lad, knock him out.'

I was throwing wild punches and shouting back at them.

'How do you fucking like that, Terry lad?' I was mimicking in a scouse accent.

It was chaos. Frank was shouting at me to shut up and focus but I wasn't listening. I didn't care about the result, I just wanted to hurt him. I couldn't let him get away with this.

It reminded me of an incident at school years earlier when a kid three years older than me had been throwing his weight around and taking the piss. I let it go for a while but the anger was building up in me.

The next day I woke up for school and went downstairs to the kitchen. I opened the knife and fork drawer and my eyes were drawn to a steak tenderiser. I picked it up and put it in my jacket. I waited all day, knowing the moment I would exact my revenge. Wayne was his name and he and all his mates would always go and sit on the swings after school and smoke dope. I had to go that way to get home anyway so took a small detour through the park. I walked up and nodded, kept my head down as if I wanted no trouble. Carefully I pulled the steak tenderiser out of my pocket and in one movement hit him right round the head. The noise was horrible and the wound opened up like a tin of beans. His mates looked at me and I stood my ground. They knew I wasn't to be fucked with now. To be honest it felt good, I liked it. I'd made my point and Wayne wouldn't be taking liberties with me again.

I never felt any guilt for the things I did – never. In my head my actions were fully justified; if people wanted to start something, I would end it.

That was how I felt about Needham and his fans now – you ruin my life, I'll ruin yours.

After the fight was over, I sat alone in the changing room, a doctor cleaning out the wound and stitching it up. There was no anaesthetic, no nothing, but I didn't care. I was still angry. A board official walked in with the 28-day ban on a piece of paper. 'Fuck off,' I said under my breath. Now I was four grand worse off and getting to the 100 was going to take even longer. It was time I didn't have.

I got a load of beers for the way home and drowned my sorrows. I'd have to lie to Vicki about the purse, tell her that I had earned a bit less than I thought. I'd say it was only twelve hundred quid instead of fifteen hundred then I could buy a bit of weed, maybe some coke. I would need all the help I could to get me through the next few weeks.

27 April 2012

Fight 82
Scott Cardle v Johnny Greaves
Echo Arena, Liverpool

I returned with a pretty easy fight against Sam Matkin up in Sheffield. Another loss, of course, but nothing I couldn't handle. What I needed was a few more of those. I couldn't cope with anything too demanding but at the same time

I needed the money and was desperate to get to the 100 quickly. That meant I would take jobs that put my health in jeopardy.

More than 80 fights in five years was too much. I hadn't boxed clever like some of the journeymen, either. I had abused myself time after time and stood in front of better men, taking a beating when I could have been sensible and covered up. At the start I was rarely dropped or stopped – now it was becoming a regular part of the game and I was getting more and more bans which, in turn, were just fuelling the dependence on drink and drugs.

Boxing had been something to distract me, a payday, but also a feeling of achievement. Now I was a shell of my former self, limping to the 100 fights. Another 20 seemed a long way off, maybe too far unless I moved quickly.

I was still outwardly brash and willing to fight anyone but deep down there was more fear. The fear of getting stopped, embarrassing myself, not achieving the only goal I had ever put my mind to. I couldn't look people in the eye if I fell short of the 100. Dad would be ashamed of me. Mum would think it was typical Johnny. Sam and Sarah would probably just laugh and not care, which was even worse. And Frank would tell me how I could have made it if I'd listened to him. I'd have to live with the regret and shame of knowing I fucked it up. Me. Nobody else. That wasn't a thought I was going to be able to live with. It would haunt me, tip me over the edge.

I had been booked to fight a lad called Scott Cardle, who had been a really top amateur. He was very well schooled and trained by Joe Gallagher, who looked after big fighters like John Murray, Anthony Crolla and the Smith brothers. If Gallagher was investing time in you then you must have some talent.

Still, in my early days I think I would have coped with him ok. He would have had more ability than me, but I would have covered up and fucked about and found a way through it. Now? Now I wasn't really sure.

The fight was taking place at the Echo Arena in Liverpool and was being broadcast by Sky. Tony Bellew was the headline, fighting against Danny McIntosh for the British light heavyweight title. Bellew was a huge name in British boxing and a massive ticket-seller. My fight was one of the main build-up bouts that would be shown live on TV.

Cardle was being touted as one of the new bright young things so there was a lot of expectation around him and how he would make that transition to the pro ranks. I had been a decent booking for his debut, in theory at least. If the promoters had watched any of my recent fights, or could see inside my head, they might have had second thoughts. There was a time when I had been that live opponent who would give him a good workout but not now. Within seconds, I knew I was way out of my depth and, for possibly the first time, I didn't want to be in that ring.

A bit like the fight against Bradley Skeete, Cardle was probably a stone heavier than me on the night. We had weighed in the day before and he had clearly stuffed his face with as much food as he could muster. He looked a lot bigger and stronger than me and was way too fit and fresh. I tried everything, all of my usual tricks. But now nothing was working. If I covered up, he peppered me with body shots and then punches to the head. If I tried to get on my bike, he would cut off the ring and corner me, landing big shots. And the punches were hurting. I don't remember the punches hurting when I first started fighting. Maybe the adrenaline wasn't there, or maybe now my body was just shot to pieces. Either way, I felt every single one and was being chased around the ring, desperately holding on.

I shipped a lot of punishment that night. Frank was desperate to pull me out but I wouldn't let him. I didn't want another 28-day ban. I couldn't cope with that.

I'm not sure how I stayed on my feet at the final bell because at one stage I think I was knocked out. I just don't remember much of the fight at all. I couldn't even remember getting dropped and at the final bell I went to the wrong corner, concussed. I was stood there asking Frank questions about how I did, totally unaware that I had been on my arse and been given one of the biggest beatings of my career.

I was never the same physically after that fight. It was like it took everything from me. They say that fighters can age overnight and that's certainly how I felt. It was just a nightmare all round really because my training partner and friend, Dan Naylor, got brutally knocked out in the most devastating manner. It would go on to be shown as one of the knockouts of the year: Dan getting caught flush on the chin and just falling face first on the canvas. Me and Frank were really worried about him for a while and stayed with him while he was checked out. In the end the doctor let us all leave and we headed back for London in Frank's BMW.

We were all feeling sorry for ourselves, including Frank, who had seen both his fighters heavily beaten and now had a long drive home. Nobody was talking but suddenly the silence was broken by the sound of a tyre popping. The car swerved a little but Frank got it under control, pulling on to the hard shoulder and swearing to himself.

We sat in the back as Frank went to assess the damage. A few minutes later he returned with the bad news:

'We ain't got a spare tyre boys, we are fucked,' he announced.

After about an hour-long wait in the dark, a low-loader arrived and took us to Birmingham to fit a spare. We ended up getting home at 9am and I can categorically say it was the worst journey of my life.

I woke up the next day feeling like I had been in an actual car crash and not a breakdown. My whole body was stiff and sore, I could barely get out of bed, my eyes were puffy and bruised, and I felt chronically dehydrated. Vicki looked at me as if to say 'what the hell happened to you?', but she knew enough not to ask too many questions. If I looked like that then it hadn't been a good night. I went to lift myself out of bed and a shooting pain threw me back on to the mattress. It was one of my ribs. I felt down and found the tender spot. The pain was worse than anything

I've ever known. A punch to the head, a baseball bat to the face. Nothing was this bad. The pain was so sharp it was like being shot. I found a way to lift myself up without putting pressure on that area and tried to go to the loo. I needed to shit but couldn't squeeze or put any pressure on that area. Every time I did, I cried out in pain.

No amount of money was worth this. I didn't want to do it anymore. My body was broken, my hands were constantly sore with blisters and cuts, I had early arthritis in my hip now and my teeth were a mess. I had lost both my front teeth and now had a replacement bridge but that kept getting broken as well. I looked an absolute state and inside I felt even worse.

My family had been pretty supportive up to this point but now they were all much more vocal about telling me to quit. Dad could see I was done and would question me about getting to 100 fights, saying it didn't matter. That just made me want to do it even more, to prove him wrong. Mum was worried and seeing me getting hurt so often was painful for her. I remember standing in her kitchen and explaining I had taken another fight as I needed the cash.

'What if something serious happens to you? Think of the kids, Johnny,' she said, with a real look of concern on her face.

I told her that I was doing it for the kids so they could be proud of their old man but that wasn't true. This was about me proving something to myself and I couldn't quit now. I would rather die in the ring than give up on the 100.

I was being selfish. None of this was fair on my family or even my opponents. They had no idea how unfit I was or how badly prepared. If something happened to me in the ring, they would have to live with that for the rest of their lives.

I felt like a bad person again. Letting everyone down, lying to people about why I was fighting, putting other people in danger but not knowing how to stop. So I was stuck and once again the voices returned. That feeling of anxiety and fear in my stomach.

I started drinking more to mask how I felt, thinking of ways I could end my life. It was a day and night fixation. There was never any respite apart from when I slept, so I would end up going to bed earlier and earlier.

It was becoming all-consuming and I wasn't being a proper partner to Vicki or father to the kids. This had to stop. So I decided to ring the doctor and book an appointment. I needed help.

He asked me one question about how I was feeling and I just blurted it all out. I told him about the drinking and drugs, the voices in my head, the suicidal thoughts and how I had come close to taking my life on a few occasions. He had clearly heard enough and put me on anti-depressants straight away. The trouble was I didn't want to take them. They made me feel broken and worthless. 'What kind of bloke needs tablets to feel ok?' I would ask myself.

I didn't want to tell anyone about my diagnosis or the medication. Dad would say not to be silly and that we all got down sometimes. Mum would have worried. Frank might have understood I suppose, but I already felt like I was putting too much on his shoulders.

I decided I had to tell Vicki though, as she would find the tablets anyway. She was upset and felt guilty for not spotting it sooner. It should have been a relief to share the problem with the person who loved me the most but it had the opposite effect. Would Vicki think I was a mess? Would she leave me now she had seen I was mentally unwell? All those thoughts went through my mind.

The pills didn't help straight away and even when they did start to have an effect, I would self-sabotage. I'd miss the odd day or decide I didn't need them anymore. All the old symptoms would return with a vengeance and the only thing that motivated me to take them was getting to the 100. If they improved me enough to get through these final few fights, then maybe they were worth it.

Chapter Fourteen

Throwing in the Towel

14 December 2012

Fight 94

Jack Catterall v Johnny Greaves
Winter Gardens, Blackpool

I was into the 90s – the final stretch. I had started out with the goal to prove something to myself. That I couldn't be stopped and was as tough as they come. That dream had long since died but one thing nobody could ever accuse me of was quitting. You could hit me and hurt me, just like Dad had done all those times, but I would never give in. I had a spirit and fight that would never be broken, no matter how bad things got. However, in a show up in Blackpool just before Christmas, I'm ashamed to say that for the first and only time in my career, I gave up.

Jack Catterall is a boxer who has become a big name in recent years and deservedly so. He clearly won his first world title fight with Josh Taylor but didn't get the decision from the judges, so I was pleased for him when he took his revenge two years later and then went on to beat Regis Prograis to become WBO champion. But for my 94th fight, and with the end in sight, he was my worst nightmare.

We had driven the six hours from London to Blackpool and arrived in plenty of time. Mickey Coveney was fighting on the same bill and we had some time to kill so we decided to go for a wander and find an off-licence. We thought we would get in the Christmas spirit early by having a little drink before the night got underway and we stuck the remaining pack of 24 cans in the boot of the car for the way home.

Mickey was fighting a future world champion in Terry Flanagan, so we were both in for a tough night. In times gone by we might have chatted about what we were going to do, how we were going to stick it on our opponent and tough it out. But life on the road had jaded both of us. Mickey was coming towards the end of his career and I was so close I could almost touch it. The Christmas break was fast approaching and neither of us had any more fights scheduled. Even if we got stopped or cut it didn't really matter as we couldn't fight for a few months anyway.

Flanagan missed the weight and was a lot bigger than Mickey, with the fight ending early. Mickey was a game lad and probably would have carried on if he had to but was looking for a way out after too many hard fights.

I felt the same. Nobody was going to shake my hand or give me a Christmas bonus for staying on my feet and toughing it out. Catterall was a classy operator without being concussive, but he caught me with a shot to the ribs that I felt and I decided to take a knee. I had never done that before in my whole career. The idea of consciously opting out of the fight just wasn't in my nature. I sucked in a few mouthfuls of breath and looked at Frank. It wasn't a big shot but I made the decision in my head: I'm staying down.

There was a time when I could never have imagined that I would do something like that. I couldn't have lived with the thought that I was a coward or a pussy. But right now, I didn't care. I stayed down and let the referee count me out. I shook my head as if I was badly hurt and took the loss.

The only thing on my mind was getting the fuck out of there and finishing up those beers on the way home. Poor Frank was designated driver as always, disappointed with the pair of us and wanting to get home as quickly as he could. But he had two pissheads in the back, laughing to ourselves and needing to stop every ten minutes so we could go for a slash. If my motivation to keep doing this was at rock bottom, that night finally broke Frank's resolve too.

27 April 2013

Fight 97
Matthew Wilton v Johnny Greaves
St Kevin's Hall, Belfast

I might have only been four fights away from retirement but if the board had had any idea about my antics they would have revoked my licence without a doubt. The drinking and lack of preparation was one thing but throwing fights was frowned upon in boxing. It went against what the sport stands for. They would look closely at things like that and come down hard on you if found guilty. A journeyman should be able to hold their own and not be a mercenary who was only there for the money and would throw himself on the floor at the first opportunity.

This was now purely about ego and getting to the 100 fights but my health was in severe jeopardy. This mission was becoming more dangerous than I had ever anticipated at the start but the more I thought about what I had become, the more I medicated with drink and drugs.

I got offered a fight at quite short notice in Belfast and, being so close to the 100, I took it without hesitation. Frank couldn't join me until the Saturday again due to work, so myself and Mickey Coveney, who was fighting on the same bill once again, went a day early for the weigh-in. Mickey was the last person that I needed accompanying me at that time because he was now in the final throes of his career and had stopped caring. We jumped on a flight together after a couple of beers at the airport to loosen us up, and headed to Northern Ireland.

Once the weigh-in was done, we got properly on the piss. There was nothing that wasn't going down our neck – Guinness, lager, wine, fags, weed, coke, vodka. You name it, we had it. I don't remember much apart from a loud banging on the door the next morning and the sound of

Frank's voice. He was already angry. I looked at the clock – it was midday. Mickey was asleep on the bed next to me, naked except for a few fag packets and empty bottles of booze. The room stank and there was mess everywhere. Fag butts, ashtrays, wine bottles, broken glasses. I looked up and noticed that we had done the old trick of taping plastic bags over the smoke alarms so they wouldn't go off. My head was banging and I could barely get up.

'Alright, alright, I'm coming,' I shouted.

I tried to put on some tracksuit bottoms and scoop up some of the mess and stick it in the bathroom. I got to the door and turned the handle but Frank's weight was already pushing it open. He looked around:

'You're a fucking disgrace John, the pair of you.'

Mickey was waking up and trying to work out what was going on. 'I've got half a mind to pull you out of the fight, fuck you John.' I was stood there half-naked, trying to defend myself like a naughty schoolboy but there was nothing I could say to make it ok.

'I'll be alright, Frank. Honestly, I'll get through it.' He looked at me with disgust and walked out. Why should he care about me if I didn't care about myself?

I sobered up as best I could but I was a shadow of my former self. I was sluggish and not fully present in the ring. I was almost thankful when another bad clash of heads stopped the fight. There was a lot of blood and a big wound. The doctor called it off and I had to have four staples in the side of my head to hold it together.

Frank barely spoke to me afterwards. There was no sympathy or compassion. I knew what he was thinking and he was right. I was an absolute liability and had no business in the ring. Thankfully the cut meant six weeks with no boxing and I devoted that period to drinking and counting down the days until I could fight again and get this done.

Three fights to go. Three too many.

15 June 2013

Fight 98

Floyd Moore v Johnny Greaves
Pyramids, Portsmouth

My first fight after the ban was a re-match with a guy I had beaten earlier in my career – Floyd Moore. He was the bloke who blew himself out after one round on his debut and I had to practically carry to the final bell. He had carved out a decent jobbing career as a fighter but wasn't pulling up any trees so I thought this might be a nice easy night's work for one of my last fights. It was down in Portsmouth at the Pyramids Centre so a nice little trip to the coast. The sun was shining but the dark clouds were circling above my head.

Frank had picked me up that morning and I was in a foul mood. I'd woken up on the wrong side of bed and just couldn't be arsed anymore. All I really wanted to do was see the kids, have a walk down to the pub and have a few pints, relax after a long week at work. Yes, I was getting a few quid for it but I knew by now that whatever we made we ended up spending. I had a bit of a thing for designer gear and me and Vicki would buy loads of smart clothes for the kids and go for a nice bite to eat. I hadn't actually made any money from all these fights, just spunked it up the wall. Having nothing to show for 97 professional fights made me feel even worse about myself. I just wanted done with the whole thing. Whatever it had once given me, it wasn't anymore.

Frank was winding me up on the way down, talking endlessly about tactics and what I needed to do.

'Frank – I don't give a fuck, mate. If I get hit, fuck it; if I get knocked out, fuck it; if I fucking die, fuck it,' I was saying.

Frank was getting more and more wound up.

'What the fuck is wrong with you, you silly cunt? What are you talking about? You've got two kids and a missus who love you, pull yourself together.'

We had a massive row on the motorway and both of us ended up sitting in silence.

Frank couldn't understand my mindset. Never could. The lack of self-care. He desperately tried to instil that in me. He would tell me how well I had done and how proud of me he was but I never felt that inside. I only got that from other people when they praised me or showed me love. Day to day I felt nothing. So I just sat staring out of the window as we got closer to Portsmouth, the sea coming into view so it almost felt like a little summer holiday. Not that either of us wanted to be there.

By the time I got to the venue, a little hall next to a swimming pool right on the seafront, I was feeling a little better. I had to weigh in first and knew I was too heavy. Fuck it, if they didn't like it I would go home. I'd stopped caring and knew I held the cards anyway. They couldn't find a replacement at that hour. No chance. I stripped down to my boxers and hopped on the scales. The bloke looked down and shifted the scales slightly, almost pushing me off before anyone could register that I was 2lb over. I have fought blokes half a stone heavier than me before so it wasn't going to matter.

I felt tired and lifeless. I grabbed a sandwich and a packet of crisps and had a lie down outside in the car. I wasn't sleeping properly and hadn't for some time. I was drinking too much and the weed probably wasn't helping either. I was depressed, taking the tablets when I remembered but frequently going weeks without and feeling suicidal again. I'd abused my body and mind for too long and this was the final painful stretch. Nothing was going to make it any easier.

The fight itself is a blur. Moore was really fired up and wanting revenge. As if it mattered. As if beating me in this state was any kind of achievement.

Frank was shouting at me to keep my guard high and slip the punches but I didn't give a fuck what happened. I'd fought Lee Selby, Anthony Crolla, Gavin Rees – proper fighters – I was fucked if I was going to cover up and let this useless sack of shit feel like he was better than me.

But he was better than me. Much better. That's how far I'd fallen. A bloke I had once toyed with and practically carried to the final bell was now beating me comfortably. I was hopeless. Throwing the odd combination, taking some heavy shots, getting cut again. I looked a mess by the end of it and Moore had his revenge. If he had known how little I cared by that point it wouldn't have meant so much to him.

I got a few cans and listened to Frank telling me where I'd gone wrong for the two-hour journey home, zoning out and descending into a lager-soaked haze.

Two fights to go. That was all I cared about. Then what? I didn't know. I just needed this to stop.

29 September 2013

Fight 99
Rakeem Noble v Johnny Greaves
York Hall, Bethnal Green

Two fights to go but the tank was running on empty. I didn't care about Rakeem Noble or putting on a show at York Hall anymore. The only thought in my mind was getting through the bout without a cut, as we had started to plan my 100th and final fight for a few weeks later and had even sold a few tickets. If I got stopped here or cut again then all that was out of the window.

Noble was making his debut and was all flashy before the fight. He jumped through the ropes in these pink silky shorts and was pulling faces at me and telling me what he was going to do. I couldn't be bothered to respond, I was that tired of boxing and all the games. He had a great physique and was clearly fit, and from the way he was moving around the ring and shadow boxing, he clearly had himself down as the next Floyd Mayweather. I just smiled to myself. I had seen all this before. The bravado. Cocky kids who had won a few amateur bouts and fancied themselves.

I usually had a bit of fun with these types of fighters but the bell sounded and I just felt like I was walking in quicksand. He wasn't heavy-handed and the shots weren't hurting, but he was picking me off almost at will. My head was snapping back as he flicked out the jab and every time I tried to ride it or step back or move my head, nothing happened. There was nothing there.

I don't want to say I was frightened because not much scared me, but it was a horrible feeling to realise that your reflexes have gone and punches are coming at you from all angles. Thank God he wasn't better or a bit sharper because I would have been stopped on my feet or knocked out, but I trudged back to the corner at the end of the first round and said to Frank:

'Fuck me, I can't lose to this cunt, he's shit.'

I sat on the stool as Frank poured water all over my face and rubbed Vaseline into my eyebrows so the punches would slip off me. He looked more serious now, Frank, and I think we were both having the same realisation. Nothing was said, just the usual advice. Get on your toes, stay on the back foot, move away from his right hand and just get through it. But something in Frank's voice let me know that he didn't believe this was possible either. Like trying to cross a road with a blindfold on, you're just praying that nothing comes your way.

I had always heard that fighters hit a point one day where they can no longer do it. In truth, that had been happening for a long time but now the needle had hit empty. I would just have to bite down on my gumshield and get through it. It was only four rounds. Four rounds and I could prepare for that final fight. But they took an eternity. Jab after jab landed, my legs feeling so heavy, Frank wiping away the blood and urging me to keep going. Eventually, the final bell came. I was nearly there. One more fight to go. But even that felt like a mountain to climb.

Chapter Fifteen

Bowing Out

29 September 2013

Fight 100

Johnny Greaves v Dan Carr
York Hall, Bethnal Green

Boxing had broken me. Or maybe I had broken myself, but I was finally on the brink of doing what I had set out to do, and the thought of all my friends and family coming to see me bow out in style got the old juices flowing for the first time in a long while.

I wanted this to be right; finishing at York Hall surrounded by the people closest to me, going out with a win and my hand held aloft. Seeing the pride on the face of my mum and dad, my brother and sister, Vicki and the kids. They had rarely seen me fight and would just hear the battle stories and see the scars. This was my final chance to show them how good I was.

I had spoken to Carl a few weeks earlier and talked him through exactly what I wanted. He managed to get me on a bill at York Hall, which was perfect as it was just down the road from where we lived so everyone could have a drink and make a night of it.

Then it was about finding the right opponent. I wanted someone tough and game but not a fighter with genuine ambition to win. This was my night, it couldn't be anyone who was too good because why would they want to fight me? Besides, I needed this to be a relatively easy night. If that was possible in the state I was in now.

We went through a load of names and then Carl suggested a lad called Dan Carr. He was available that night and fitted the journeyman mould – at that point he had only won four of his 42 fights so he was the right type – but I had seen Dan around the circuit a bit and he was a tough kid. I mean, we all were or we wouldn't be able to make a living like this, but he wasn't someone who would stand and have a tear-up. I liked the idea of going out on my shield, swinging punches Rocky-style and getting my hand raised with a face covered in blood. But Dan wasn't that guy. He was slippery and clever and knew how to cover up and not get hit. He didn't often go to war and if we did go for him then it might be quite a boring fight for the fans. That worried me a bit. Dan was awkward and proud and would make my life difficult. But surely he would know it was my final fight and would go easy, know his place? As it was, we didn't really have any choice because there weren't a whole lot of options. So Dan was booked as the opponent and York Hall was sorted too.

The week of that final fight I trained harder than I ever had. I acted like a proper professional for the first time in my career because I was terrified. Terrified of letting myself down and getting beaten in front of all those people. I couldn't let that happen. In my head that really mattered. If I lost then everyone would think less of me.

As well as working and training every night down at the Peacock with Frank, I was also trying to sell the 100 tickets I had asked the promoter for. I'd promised him I would have a big following but it was a massive pain in the arse. I was calling and checking in on people, trying to collect the dough and keep track of it all. In the end Frank, who was always better at maths than me, agreed to take over the operation and let me concentrate on the fight.

I was spending the whole time thinking about it, picturing everyone there, on their feet at the end when they announced my name as the winner. Being carried out of the ring and Dad and all his mates buying me drinks back at the working men's club. It was going to be the night of my life, as long as I had enough left to win.

I didn't even drink much that week. Maybe just the odd can before bed. Between thoughts of the fight, I would drift off and start considering life after boxing. That scared me. I had no idea what I would do or how I would survive. Financially and emotionally boxing had always given me some sort of lift. Even in the bad times, feeling something was better than feeling nothing.

It was a Sunday afternoon show so I woke early and knocked about with the kids for a bit but my mind was on the fight. I wanted to get to York Hall and get myself sorted, so I left early, getting a cab over there and feeling those butterflies for the final time as I approached the venue. That was especially true somewhere like York Hall with so much history and somewhere that had been so special for me.

I wandered up with my bag over my shoulder and the security guard recognised me. 'You fighting today?' 'Last one,' I replied. 'My 100th fight and then I'm done.' 'No way,' he said and gave me a big hug. The place was empty apart from people getting the ring ready so I wandered around and had a look. I remembered my fight there back in the unlicensed game and I imagined what it would look and feel like later when it was packed, seeing Mum and Dad, Vicki and the kids. I kept getting emotional and had to keep reminding myself I still had a fight to get through.

There were three or four fights on before me. I'd sold a lot of tickets so, although I wasn't the headline, I would be on quite late when the arena was full. That meant I had to sit backstage and wait and it seemed to take an age. Fighters coming and going, Frank wrapping my hands and getting me ready. I was trying to focus on the fight ahead but every time I thought about stepping through the curtain, my name announced, seeing all those people I knew for the final time, I would well up. I needed to get a grip.

Eventually one of the organisers came in and told me I was on next. I felt weak. Like I'd invested so much emotional energy into the day already. Then I started to worry again about being stopped or knocked out. The looks on everyone's faces. Having to leave without a drink or pat on the back. My career ending in the worst way possible. 'Johnny, Johnny!' Frank was splashing water on my face and shouting at me to man up. I heard Dan Carr being introduced to the crowd and a few boos. I smiled to myself and imagined my mates getting involved.

'Is Vicki and the kids here? Where are they sitting? What about Mum and Dad?' I asked.

Frank reassured me and told me to switch on for the final time.

I made my way to the edge of the dressing room and waited for the ring announcer – Simon Goodall – to introduce me. I had a little look out and could see it was rammed. The lights were dark and only the stage was all lit up. A little shiver went through me. This was my time.

'Ladies and gentlemen,' began the MC. 'Tonight is a very special night for one of the real characters of British boxing. This evening he will take part in his 100th professional fight before bowing out. Will you please put your hands together for one final time, the pride of East Ham, Johnnnnnnnnnny Greaves!'

There were tears running down my cheeks. I dabbed them away with my gloves and got ready to walk to the ring. I heard the familiar opening chords of 'Cigarettes and Alcohol' by Oasis, my theme tune, and swaggered out to a huge ovation. People I didn't know were cheering, I could see mates on their feet. As I turned and headed for the ring I looked to my left and there was Sam and Sarah, applauding and grinning. Mum and Dad were behind them, stood together. I choked up for a second, gave them a little smile and stepped through the ropes. 'Dad, Dad!' I looked down and there was Ted and Ruby, jumping up and loving the whole thing. 'I love you,' I mouthed and blew them a kiss. Fuck. This was overwhelming. I was struggling to stop the tears, the feeling of pride, and of something even less familiar. What was that? Then I recognised it – happiness. I felt happy and content. They had all come to see me. Johnny.

Then I caught sight of Dan Carr. He looked unimpressed and was staring. Any thoughts I might have had about an easy night soon disappeared. He looked fit and well, ready to cause an upset. I inhaled and the referee brought us together to give us our instructions. From the first bell to the last, all I remember is the noise. Hearing all the voices I knew cheering and pleading with me to win. Every punch I landed received a huge cheer. When Dan did have his moments there were boos and jeers. He was the pantomime villain and I was the crowd favourite or hero.

He was frustrating me just as I knew he would. Dan was good enough to win plenty of fights. He was just another journeyman who had chosen that life rather than sell tickets. He was game, and the more the crowd insulted him the harder he fought. He was ducking and weaving and looking to throw counter shots. I was just going all out, fighting on emotion. Throwing wild punches and going through the repertoire. I would have loved to have knocked him out or stopped him, and maybe a few years earlier I might have done. But the snap had gone from my shots and he was never really in trouble, although I was confident I had done enough to win on points.

The final round was a real ding-dong. I was throwing the kitchen sink at him, he was slipping and throwing back, we were both landing shots and the crowd were loving it. The final bell went and I fell into his arms. The referee took a moment to weigh things up and then raised my hand in victory. I just lost it. Ted and Ruby ran into the ring and I had them in my arms, tears streaming down my face. 'Johnny, Johnny!' the crowd were chanting. Mum and Dad were on their feet, Vicki was in tears. The whole thing felt like a dream. This didn't happen to me. Not Johnny Greaves. Good things never came my way.

We headed back to the working men's club and I can honestly say it was the best night of my life. Surrounded by friends and family, all the people I loved, just an outpouring of love and respect. Anyone who doubted what I did had now seen how tough it was. Anyone who thought I was just a loser had now seen me win. We sat there until the early hours laughing and drinking, me the centre of attention for once, loving the limelight. After 100 fights, I was done.

Chapter Sixteen

After the Lights Go Out

I WOKE up the following morning and I wasn't a boxer anymore. I was just plain old John Greaves again. Painter, partner, father. Another bloke in the street trying to look after his family and make an honest living. And for a while that felt enough.

Boxing had given me so much but also taken a lot from me. I had started off with a dream, an idea of what boxing was and what it would do for me. It was going to be a place where I could prove my toughness. A place that I could escape to and be someone else for a while. A place where I could feel pain. The kind of pain I felt on the inside every day.

For a while boxing was that place but it wore me down to the point that I stopped caring. The long road trips and late-night journeys home. The loneliness of being the away fighter with no support. The abuse of the crowd and the lack of respect. The cuts and bruises. The politics of the game that meant you would always be a loser no matter how well you fought. I'd grown sick and tired of it all.

I'd like to say that reaching the 100 fight mark gave me the closure that I needed but of course it didn't. I quickly forgot the pain and hardship of the final year as a professional. I remembered only the good parts and erased the rest. I started to feel lost without it. I longed to feel that adrenaline rush again. Nothing in normal, everyday life could compare to that. I loved my kids but I was nothing without boxing.

Many times I thought about stepping through the ropes again. I would convince myself I could do it, that we needed the cash, that maybe things might be different this time. But thankfully Frank or Vicki talked me out of it. I was done. I was an ex-boxer. I knew that really. I was just scared of what life might look like without it.

I wished that I could feel pride at what I'd achieved but most of the time I just felt like a loser. I would go over the things in my mind that I should have done differently, how I had wasted my talent.

I kept going to the gym every now and then, hitting the bags or having a little spar, but what was the point now? I enjoyed being around the fighters though and started training a couple of journeymen. I would pass on what I had learned and try to teach them all the things that I had never done. Train well, cover up, look after yourself, don't get hit. There was a certain irony to that, which wasn't lost on me.

It made me realise that Johnny Greaves had only ever been a mask really. I was always 'John boy' growing up. He was sad and sensitive and negative. Johnny was different. He was confident and flashy and funny and didn't give a fuck. I invented Johnny because I didn't like John. But he was dead now and I was back to the old me.

It was so hard without boxing but I needed to find a way to live and be happy. I still frighten myself a lot. My thoughts scare me. My depression will never be fully under control and I'm still taking the tablets but I don't want to be on them forever. I love Vicki and the kids but often think their life would be better without me. Do I really want to be here for the next 30 or 40 years? I don't know. If suicide wasn't so impactful on people around you I would have taken that leap. I don't enjoy life and never have.

Retirement was already hard enough, then in late 2018 Dad announced that he wasn't well. He had changed a lot down the years, mellowed into a softer person. But he still had that bravado about him and said he would be fine.

A little while later he announced out of the blue that he had prostate cancer and it had spread into his lymph nodes and beyond. It was a death sentence but Dad seemed unperturbed.

'We all die at some point, I'm alright John boy.'

He wasn't sure how long he had left and didn't want any fuss, typical Dad. The doctors told him if he lived a healthy life, gave up the booze and fags and took his diet seriously, then he might have a few more years but Dad wanted to enjoy himself and keep drinking with his mates.

I was already struggling to adjust and to find hope in anything, and Dad's news sent me into the deepest depression of my life. I had stopped taking the tablets, desperate to stand on my own two feet. I would go from feeling tired and irritable to bouts of severe paranoia. Christmas with Vicki's family turned into a nightmare after I became convinced her dad and brother-in-law were talking about me behind my back.

Vicki tried to arrange a holiday to Cornwall, just us and the kids, but I couldn't bear to go. I didn't have the strength and just wanted to sit at home and drink. Then I would feel selfish and hate myself even more, so the cycle became even worse.

One night Vicki let it all pour out, telling me she feared I was going to get sectioned if I carried on acting like this. How every phone call she received frightened her because she thought it would be the police telling her they had found my body.

And that's when we headed to Norfolk. A final chance to find happiness as a family, ending with me on a clifftop preparing to jump. When I got back to the hotel room that night, my trousers covered in mud and sand, I just collapsed into Vicki's arms. The kids had always seen my mood swings and they knew I suffered with depression but they finally understood how serious the situation was. I saw how worried they were about me and it made me feel even worse. How could I put them through this? Ruby was telling me that I didn't mean it. She felt as though me coming back was a good sign, a sign that I wouldn't follow through on my actions. Ted was older and maybe understood me a little better. He didn't want to sleep, in case I did something, and we had to talk to him for a long time and reassure him it was all ok before he allowed himself to drift off.

Seeing the reaction of the kids that night and witnessing the strength that Dad was showing in his battle should have given me a greater appreciation for life but mental illness doesn't work that way. In many ways it made me feel even lower.

I wasn't afraid of death and neither was Dad. We were both facing very different battles to survive – his physical and mine mental. The only time I saw him upset was about a month before he passed. He had lost a lot of weight and become very sick. He was called into hospital so I went with him for support. After the check-up he was having a consultation and misheard the doctor, thinking he was going to die that night. He just broke down in front of me for the first time in his life. I had never seen him show any sign of vulnerability but here he was, crying and telling me he was afraid. I had no idea what to do beyond hold him and tell him it was going to be ok. But we both knew it wasn't going to be ok for long.

A few months passed and Dad was getting progressively worse. He needed round-the-clock help, with me and Frank taking turns to stay with him. We would have to try to get him in and out of the shower and even clean him up after a shit. It was degrading for him and he would talk a lot about wanting to die.

'How long have I got to wait, John boy?'

It was no kind of life for him anymore. He was unrecognisable from the man we grew up with, physically and emotionally. It was like he didn't have to put on an act anymore and all the things he had bottled up throughout his life, things he was afraid to say, suddenly spilled out. He would tell me how proud he was of me and how much he loved me.

One night I had finished work and was just settling down for the night when the phone went. It was Frank. He was with Dad and said that he was asking for me. I told him that I would have some dinner and then pop over for a bit.

Frank was with him when I arrived, the old man lying on the settee that we had turned into a bed for him. It saved him going up and down the stairs. He was comfortable there and could watch TV and sleep when he needed to. He looked very pale and weak but a bit happier in himself. Maybe the medication was kicking in. He thanked me for coming and told me to go and get a special bottle of brandy he had kept under the sink. I got the bottle and three glasses and we all sat together, slowly getting pissed and talking about the old days. We were laughing our heads off. Dad was reminiscing one second, then he would get emotional, then there would be a one-liner. It was the most lucid I had seen him for months. He was remembering all these details about holidays and life when we were kids. It was like having the old Dad back for a night, or maybe an even better version. We got through the brandy and whatever else we could find and at some point in the night we must have fallen asleep in the sitting room together.

I woke up feeling a bit the worse for wear and went next door to put the kettle on. My head was banging but I had a little warm glow about me. It had been a great night with the three of us together. I walked back into the living room and gave Frank a nudge. I'd let Dad sleep. He needed the rest. But something was different. He looked pale and still. I walked over and put my hand on his forehead. He was cold. I checked for a pulse. Nothing. Frank and I looked at each other and knew. He was gone. It was like he had felt the end was coming and wanted one last night with his sons.

We just sat with him for a while and cried. This man who had shaped my life in so many ways, good and bad. He had been my nemesis and my hero. Someone I was terrified of yet wanted his approval. I could have felt anger towards him, maybe even relief that he was gone. But all I felt was love and sadness. He was my dad. Any beating he had given me I deserved. He was the man who taught me how to survive, how to be tough. I owed him my life. In many ways I was a man in his mould – a fighter, a provider, a survivor. I'm proud to say I never hit a woman in my life but apart from that, me and Dad weren't that different. I miss him every day.

Writing this book has been a painful experience for me. My life has been a struggle from day one and continues to be today. I'm worried that I'll sound like an East End gangster or someone who glorifies fighting, drinking and taking drugs. I don't at all and I hope that my kids will read this and understand.

I'm ashamed of so many things that I did. I should have respected myself so much more, respected boxing more, made better choices and looked after my health better and my family financially. I should have been a better partner to Vicki, a better brother to Frank, a better father to Ted and Ruby. But I promise, I did my best. I was only ever trying to stay alive. If my decisions and behaviour looked selfish, then I'm sorry.

I am proud of my toughness and for having 100 professional fights but I'm not a hard man, I'm a deeply flawed human being. Everything I've done has been to mask the feeling that I'm worthless. That I have no value. The drinks and the drugs just helped me to forget that for a while. It was stupid and dangerous to do what I did and I would never condone or make light of some of my actions before or after fights. The fact I'm still here and breathing is a miracle, even if I can't appreciate the beauty of being alive. Maybe one day I will. Maybe the process of writing this book might just help a little bit too.

Thank you for reading this: you don't know how grateful I am. To everyone I let down, I'm sorry. To my dad, rest easy big man. Mum – you're always in my heart. Frank – thank you so much. Vicki, Ted and Ruby – I love you forever.

Johnny x